THE CHARADE NIGHT CLUB

The Untold Story

The DJs inside the Pendulum club circa 1967

Published by ACM Retro Ltd,
The Grange,
Church Street,
Dronfield,
Sheffield S18 1QB.

Visit ACM Retro at:
www.acmretro.com

Keith Brisland asserts the moral right to be identified
as the author of this work.

A catalogue record for this book is available from the British Library.

THE CHARADE NIGHT CLUB

The Untold Story

**The Charade crowd on a Bank
Holiday in Scarborough**

**Matchy and colleague practicing backdrops
outside Manchester's Twisted Wheel**

Contents

Chapter 3 - A new Decade, the '80s

Foreword

Having read the manuscript there is no doubt about it, Keith Brisland has certainly spent some man hours researching the background for his book.

It brings back memories, most of them good. The Charade operated in a time when people went out to really enjoy themselves, dress fashionably and acted sensibly and good times were had by all.

Many of the names and incidents in the book bring back happy memories and I am pleased to see that many of the then clients have gone on to make a name for themselves.

For me the Charade was where it all started and it's been a long and mostly enjoyable journey.

Enjoy the read.

Dave Allen

Dave Allen (centre) at his Josephines' venue

INTRODUCTION

This is the story of a nightclub. It is a story of music, personalities and a small, unlikely corner of South Yorkshire that was at the cutting edge of the music scene for eighteen years.

The nightclub was the Charade. Its owner was Dave Allen who was forced to put up his home as collateral when he bought the club's lease in 1968. He went on to build an entertainment empire – ran from offices tucked away at the back of the Charade's dance floor – that would eventually be worth over £60 million. We will hear from the people who made the Charade as famous in its day to the teenagers of Rotherham as the Beatles and the Rolling Stones. DJs from Eric Dewsnap and Melvyn 'Speedy' Kaye to Sean Hampsey and Neil 'Noddy' St John give the lowdown on the venue and look at how it helped shaped a number of different music scenes from the 1960s charting the rise and fall of Tamla Motown, Progressive Rock, Punk Rock, Disco and the New Romantics. We will hear how they the DJs learnt their trade, and in particular learn more about Rick Stuart who mixed three number one hit singles for Jive Bunny and worked as a Radio One producer alongside Bruno Brookes, Mark Goodier and Paul Gambaccini.

There are first-hand accounts from the people who used to work for Allen at the Charade such as Mick Bradford, Dave Growns and John Rose. And we will learn about Allen's involvement with Foreign Secretary William Hague's family who used to supply the drinks to the Charade and his growing nightclub business.

It is a story that describes the evolution of Northern Soul, of night time trips across the country to Wolverhampton, Manchester and Stoke on Trent, the All England Dancing Competition, drugs, jail sentences, Formula One, mayors and chief constables.

In short it is a story of a South Yorkshire icon and the people who made it what was.

Chapter 1

The Early Years

Dave Allen, a former Jazz band leader, bought the Charade nightclub in 1968. Almost penniless, he had to put his house on the line to raise enough money and persuade the bank to take a risk. Forty years later he had become one of the country's wealthiest individuals, making it to 944 on The Sunday Times Rich List of 2006; worth over £60 million. This is the story of that first night club, told by the people who worked for Allen and the punters who flocked through the doors every week, it follows the changing music scene from the swinging sixties through to the mid '80s and describes an industrial Yorkshire town's love affair with the Charade.

The Charade first opened its doors as a jazz club on the 15th August 1968. A year later the Woodstock Festival opened on the 15th August 1969. The first owner of the Charade was Nobby Clarke from Doncaster who previously had been a deep sea diver. The club was located above the Fine Fare supermarket on the Stag Roundabout, in a residential area on the edge of the town centre. Barry Cryer who went that very first night with his wife and friends describes walking up those legendary narrow stairs into a very small and intimate club.

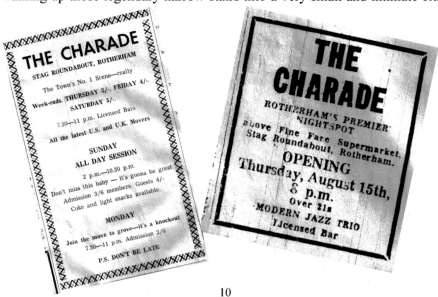

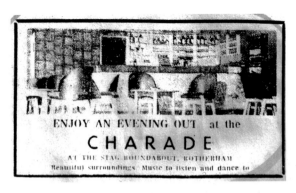

ENJOY AN EVENING OUT at the
CHARADE
AT THE STAG ROUNDABOUT, ROTHERHAM
Beautiful surroundings. Music to listen and dance to

"There were wooden planks placed over trestle tables acting as a make shift bar, similar to a barn dance setting, with a few tables and chairs scattered about, it gave you the impression of being very unprofessional, in the far corner was the dance floor with a piano next to it and also a place for someone to play records". The dance floor was described in an advertisement as being half the size of a ballroom dance floor and parking was limited at the moment but underground parking for up to 36 cars would soon be available beneath the supermarket.

The club was licensed for 150 people and the bar had to close at 10.30pm, the same as all the public houses. Barry goes on to say "he heard a few people saying how they were disappointed, it was not what they had expected from a Jazz Club", with people wandering over to the Stag public house for a drink and then coming back in later. The windows that ran down one side of the club and looked out onto the main road were not blacked out, as they were later on and it seemed odd having a night club with natural light flooding in.

It was advertised as a Modern Jazz Club, mainly playing live Jazz with Jazz records between sets. Some of the early Jazz groups to appear there were;

The Mike Paterson Trio, playing most Fridays and Saturdays, with Mod dancing on Saturday nights.

The Mike Shore Jazz Band, whose first session there on 29th August 1968, has been taped, their first number being 'Precious Lord Lead Me On' and the last one being, 'I Want A Little Girl'.

Jenette and the Modest Five were also another well known jazz group to appear at the weekends. In the week they would mainly play records with their resident DJ.

Dave Allen a trumpet player and band leader at the Mecca dance hall in Sheffield had heard about the Charade playing the latest style of Jazz called Trad Jazz. He explained how one evening he had a meeting with Nobby Clarke and remembers asking him "how well is the club doing at the weekends? "Not as profitable as I had hoped for" came back the reply. We now see a true entrepreneur in action, Dave replies, "why not let me run a disco for a few weekends, I'll take the money on the door and you can keep the entire bar takings". Eventually they agreed to try it for a month or so.

The Charade along with other venues in the area was being used by Dave Allen and his partner John Stead, (the sax player in the same band as Dave) to run dances. They would hire the venue, bring in the DJ and sound system if required, see to the promotional side of things and at the end of the night keep the profits.

They carried out extensive flyer dropping for the next few weeks, advertising the Charade wherever they were working. As Dave vividly remembered "the very first night they were queuing in their hundreds outside the club, past all the shops and down the road". Teenagers from around the area would be rushing home from work, having a quick wash and something to eat, before dashing to join the queue. One such young person was Andy Bell, who can remember that if you arrived after 7.30pm you would not get in.

It was a great success and after a few weekends Dave said "I asked Nobby what he thought of our joint venture, 'Can't stand the music' he said 'and in any case I'm thinking of selling the club and moving on'". I then asked him how much he wanted for the club. 'You can't afford it', he told me, but after I probed him further, he said 'over £ 3000'."

So for the next few weeks Dave and John went around their families and friends to raise enough money to buy the club. Eric Dewsnap remembers going over to Dave's house one Sunday afternoon, he goes on to explain, "He was offered a lease on the Charade and it was a tough one to call, since they did not have the money, which meant that Dave had to put his house up as collateral". When they asked him for his opinion about taking on the lease he replied "it would be like minting money". Eric also remembers that they were great promoters and took it from a few people attending to packed houses every weekend.

This was the very beginning with his partner John Stead of A and S Leisure Group, which within three years would become the area's largest entertainment company, eventually growing into a multi million pound entertainment group, with night clubs, casinos, dog tracks and Dave Allen becoming chairman of

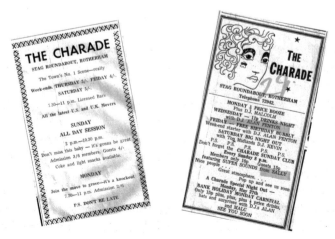

Sheffield Wednesday football club in their portfolio. By 2006 A&S Leisure employed over 700 people across the UK.

Eric Dewsnap DJ

Born in Greasbrough in 1948, Eric went to Wingfield Comprehensive School where he passed 5 GCEs. After leaving school he found employment at Backer Electric as a Technical Apprentice making Heating Elements, he describes the company, "it was a medium sized company in the town and employed about 500 people, mostly women making heating elements and we were located on the Eastwood Trading Estate opposite the KP, nut factory".

In 1963 he visited his first pop concert when he went to see the Beatles at the City Hall in Sheffield on the 16th March with Chris Montez and Tommy Roe heading the bill and from that day on "I was hooked by music". When the same tour reached Edinburgh they had a far different reception to the one in Sheffield, as one young female fan described on the radio "a girl friend from school told me about the concert, so we got tickets and went along. When the Beatles came on, who by the way were 3rd billing the entire audience stood up as one and screamed. When the main act of the evening Chris Montez came on he took off his jacket, then he took off his tie, then he started to unbutton his shirt, then the entire audience rushed the stage and stripped him. In those days there was no security only an old caretaker with a mop and bucket trying to help him and shouting I'll tell your mums. My only regret is that we didn't rush the stage when the Beatles were on".

In 1965 a close friend of Eric's, filled in an application form in his name for a trainee DJ at the Heart Beat club in Sheffield without telling him. It was advertised in the Sheffield Star. "I was determined to have the last laugh on him, so I went along for the interview and somehow talked my way into the job, I was only 17 years old at the time. I was working with David Hamilton, who was known to everybody as Diddy David Hamilton, a name given to him by Ken Dodd. He would go on to be a TV and radio presenter and so for the next nine months he taught me all there was to know on how to be a top DJ. We always finished at two in the morning with the club putting on a special taxi to take me home to Wingfield, I would then be working the same morning at Backer Electric making heating elements. Once I had finished my apprenticeship I had the knowledge and skills from work to start my own company called "Series Sound" making and always improving the equipment a DJ would need. Within a couple of years we had ten mobile discos on the road most nights and since we were one of only two companies in the country doing this we were getting bookings from Newcastle to the north of London".

At the age of 19 Eric is a regular visitor on his scooter to Sheffield's legendary Mojo Club where he was fortunate to see most of the artists and groups of the period perform. He reminds all music lovers in his own words, "The music scene in South Yorkshire owes a great gratitude to Peter Stringfellow, he was the person who had the foresight and vision to travel down to London every few weeks to bring back as yet, unheard American records to play in the clubs up here. Without him the soul scene in the late '60s would not have been as vibrant as it became". When news reaches the clubs in the north of England about the up and coming Stax Road Show, with Otis Redding topping the bill, Eric decided to get more than one ticket. "Rather than go to Leeds to see the show I decided to drive over the Pennines to Manchester and buy 48 tickets with my own money from the box office, I can still remember the look on their faces when I asked for 48 tickets at the same time as handing over the money. Once back home all I had to do now was hire a coach and sell the tickets, which I did at the local YMCA".

So as Dave Allen and John Stead took over the ownership of the Charade they turned to Eric to be one of their regular DJs. Eric has fond memories of the club "I really liked the layout inside with that very low ceiling which gave it great acoustics and atmosphere, if the club had been twice as big we could have still filled it. After 18 months I'd built up a great repartee within the club mainly playing pop and soul music". He now explains how the Co-op night club, which was 300 yards away from the Charade in a sports and social club built by the Co-op supermarket started. "One weekend I arrived about 20 minutes late to find all my records at the bottom of the stairs with Dave Allen, I was informed that my services were not required any more due to the fact that I was late. No matter how much I explained, Dave was not having any of it and

Heavy Sounds

An application by Series Sound for permission to run progressive music sessions in the Town Hall's Howard Room has been granted by Rotherham Borough Council.

Subject to the hall not being required in connection with bookings for the main Assembly Rooms, Series Sound are to be allowed the use of the plush Howard Room on a week by week basis.

Attendances at the sessions will be limited to 80.

THE

CHARADE

STAG ROUNDABOUT,
ROTHERHAM

The Town's
Premier Nite Spot

FULLY LICENSED TILL
12 MIDNIGHT

★

SUPER SATURDAY. — Excitement London Style with Yorkshire's No. 1 DJ Dave Growns. Your chance to win two Giant Teddy Bears for just 30p. Just save your admission tickets.

P.S.—Watch out for Christmas programme.

gave me my week's wages. By this time word had got around the club what was happening downstairs, so now well over half of the club voted with their feet and went across the road to the Stag pub".

With well over 100 hundred loyal followers wondering what to do next, Eric hit on a new plan "I decided to take every one over to the Co-op since I knew they had a band on that weekend, it was the type of band that mum and dad would get up to dance to, like an upmarket Working Men's Club. As we all arrived at the door I handed over my weeks wages and said to the doorman, let in as many as this money will pay for?". The doorman noticed well over 100 hundred teenagers queuing up and replied 'you can all come in free' and that was the first night ever that the Co-op dance floor rocked. That same night Oscar, the club's secretary, offered me the job as their DJ".

The following weekend the Co-op had become a rival to the Charade on Friday and Saturday nights since they were playing the same type of music. Eric paid tribute to Jock Anderson another DJ, "it was Jock who started to play more and more rock based music with less emphasis' on the dance type music that was being played at the Charade", so within a few months the Stag Roundabout had two night clubs at the weekends, but both catering for opposing tastes in music. One advantage that the Co-op had over the Charade is that it had its own Cricket field at the back where people could wander over to at the end of the night and did. After working one night at the Charade in August of 1969 Eric remembers a peculiar thing with the police, "I was driving up to the Brecks in my sports car when in my mirror I saw the blue flashing lights from a police car. They pulled me over and one of the officers came over and said, "I'd recognise your sports car anywhere Eric, anyway did you know there's a great band on at the Penthouse tomorrow night? You'd better get yourself over there". The following night Eric and his crowd from the Charade were watching the Progressive Rock Band (Yes), at the Penthouse, courtesy of the police. The very next day they released their eponymous debut LP "Yes".

Like most of the DJs in the early years at the Charade he often found himself working at another one of Dave Allen's clubs in Dewsbury called the Bin Lid. This was a coffee bar with a large dance floor upstairs where Dave Allen would put on regular All Night Dances, (all-nighters). On one such night Eric found himself as the DJ and compere for Ike and Tina Turner.

In the early '70s Eric had the pleasure of working alongside Yes at The Engineers Ball held annually at Leeds University, "I was the person that had made and operated by hand the stride scopes. In those early days I would make two circular discs out of clear Perspex; then I would place a seal between them, partially filling the gap with a coloured liquid before finally closing the seal.

I would then mount this into a piece of wood, then all I had to do on the night was spin the disc and at the same time shine a strong light through it, this gave a psychedelic feel to the concert".

Ron Stanley DJ

Ron started as a DJ while working as an apprentice engineer at Firth Vickers in Sheffield and went to the Brecks Community Centre which ran a weekly youth club for local teenagers in the area. It was owned by Dalton Parish Council who continue to own it to this day. The only advertisement for the Brecks Youth Club is from the 10th June 1967. It advertises a disco in the woods, which surround two thirds of the building, then indoors if it rains. When he first started going to the club there were about 20 teenagers inside, with a few of them dancing to the records being played, so he asked Nigel Gimiva who was running the club "why not let me try playing my records and see if I can get more people in, since he's not doing a very good job". After a few weeks of being the resident DJ, word had got around that the place to be on a Wednesday and Friday nights was the Brecks Youth Club. Ron goes on to say "I decided to give the club a name and after a lot of thinking I came up with the name The Detroit Wheel, because of the connection with Detroit and Tamla Motown". It was also the car manufacturing capital of America, hence the Wheel in the name. Within a few weeks he had hundreds of teenagers turning up, with a large proportion coming from further afield on their scooters. Since the Community Centre is at the end of a very quiet residential road its days were numbered, but Ron explains, "I could see the potential for a club in the area giving teenagers the music that they wanted to dance to, because of the atmosphere the music was creating in such clubs as the Mojo in Sheffield and The Pendulum in Rotherham town centre". But alas the Parish Councillors at the time were short-sighted and prevented the youth club from becoming a major outlet for teenagers at night. In Ron's words "it was like a June frost, killing the tender shoots of aspiring teenagers". As one door closes another one opens for our young entrepreneur.

While having a drink one night in the Stag pub, he decided to pay a visit to the Charade Jazz Club across the road. On entering the premises he noticed it was not very busy with the few people inside dancing to old time music or the waltz, he explained "to me they were dancing like my mum and dad would have danced". He goes on to say "I introduced myself to Jerry Clarke and his wife and asked if they would be interested in running a dance on a Friday night?" "No came back the answer, we are not interested in that type of music". On his way out he left them his telephone number; just in case they changed their minds. They did change their minds and gave Ron a chance, but due to a lack of advertising not many people were turning up.

Ron was also one of the resident DJs at another well known night club in the town centre called the UP N UP, this club first opened its doors on the 10th of November 1967, on a Friday night. It was located in the Co-op building on Westgate. This was one of the first clubs in the town to be licensed and opened from 8pm until midnight. Dave Allen looked on the club as his main competitor when he first took over the Charade. It ran for about two and a half years altogether. Ron remembers those first few weeks with the records jumping on the decks, "because the dance floor was a wooden tongue and groove construction, the record decks would bounce when everybody was dancing, causing the needle to jump on the records. We eventually came up with the idea of suspending the twin decks on wire ropes hung from the ceiling".

It was given the name Up N Up because you went up a lot of stairs to where the Co-op cafe was located. The club became so popular, with room inside for only 250 people that it had to introduce a membership scheme to stop the hundreds of disappointed teenagers queuing every Friday night and not being able to get in. Bob Holyman and his friends can remember

THE
CHARADE
STAG ROUNDABOUT
HERRINGTHORPE
Where the action is!!

Hey Babe, you've tried
the rest — now try this

FRIDAY and
SATURDAY
A REAL FUNKY
DANCIN' SCENE.
7.30-11.30. Admission 5/-
Licensed Bars, Over 18s

MONDAY
THE SATIN SOUL
SHOW
7.30-10.30. Admission 2/6
A real Gas Nite

THURSDAY
Sock it to mi one more
time, Babe.
7.30-10.30. Admission 3/-

SATURDAY
MORNING
10 a.m.-12 noon
JUNIOR DISC
SESSION
6-14-years-old
Pops and Party Dances
Admission 2/-
All session compered
by Eric and Ronnie

P.S. Don't be late
Saturday Nite.

Available for private
functions Tuesday and
Wednesday evenings.
and Wedding Receptions
Saturday afternoon.
Phone Sheffield 388289.

queuing and at the same time trying to hide from his cousin Dave Brown. He'd always come looking up and down the queue for younger teenagers that he knew, on the scrounge "can you lend us sixpence Bob?" he would ask. Bob remembers, "I'd always say no - I knew if I handed it over I'd never see that sixpence again". But no wasn't enough for him: "I'd have to turn out all my pockets and even take my shoes off, just to show him how much I had for myself".

The plus side of this was, Bob goes on to say, "Once in the club, no one bothered me because they knew Big Dave was my cousin, he ran a friendly protection racket".

So where did our young DJs get to hear the records they would eventually be playing at their clubs before everyone else had heard them?
One such place was Brittain's furniture store. Upstairs where the cafe was located was the records counter and running down one side of the wall there were four record booths, each one the size of a red phone box. This is where, on a Friday afternoon the DJs would congregate to listen to all the latest record releases for that week. They would then pick the ones they hoped the teenagers would dance to that night in their clubs. There was also the record counter at Boots on High Street, but here the booths only came over your head, with only two heads fitting inside each booth, while at Brittain's you could squeeze at least four people into a booth.
But Ron was one step ahead of all the other DJs in as much as he had a relation living in New York. He goes on to explain, "After reading the musical papers and magazines, especially 'Blues and Soul' each week I would write to my relation in New York requesting certain records to be sent over". One record he remembers was The Champions part 1 and 2 by Willie Mitchell. "I would send them a list by Airmail, not email as we do now, and so on average it would take about three to four weeks from reading about a new release to actually playing it in the clubs".
A lot of records at this time would first be released in America and then if at all months later in the UK. British groups did the same but the other way round, i.e. first released in the UK and then secondly in America.

Once Dave Allen had started to run dances with Jerry, the owner of the Charade it was only natural for Ron to work for A and S Dance Promotions as it was then called. Like most of the early Charade DJs, Ron also went on to work at other clubs owned by A and S, which included the Bin Lid at Dewsbury, the Purple Haze at Chesterfield and the Birdcage at Hoyland.
Ron would sit and plan his record play-order before going on. He explains why "you could only build the atmosphere on the dance floor up to a peak twice in one night" and this had the down side that he found it hard to fit in a record request from someone who came into the club late. "This happened to me at The Birdcage one night", he explained, "someone came and asked me for a record that I'd just played, later on he came and asked again, I told him I'd already played it, so he turned and walked away, two minutes later an empty pint pot came flying over my head, you had to be able to duck quickly working

there", while the pint pot would be caught in the fishing nets strung behind the DJ.

Ron would often roll in at home between midnight and 4 am; this was partially due to Dave Allen taking him and other members of the staff out for a meal when the club had closed at night. He goes on to describe one such night in particular "Dave took us all to a Chinese restaurant in Sheffield one night after we'd closed up at the Charade. It was the first time most of us had been to such a place and what made it stand out was that the session act was an unknown Labi Siffre", who became an influential singer/song writer and poet.

Over time Ron had built up a large record collection, he reminisces "I used to carry all my records for the night in an old suitcase that my parents gave me, which I still have. Before I could drive I had to catch the bus into town every Friday night with my suitcase full of records, while I was working at the Up N Up, I dread to think what the regulars on that seven o'clock bus thought, but working at the Charade allowed me to walk to work, so I could sometimes leave my records there". While working for A and S at private functions he would often have to rely on a friend from work dropping him off and then picking him up when he had finished working. On one occasion his work colleague decided to spend the evening with him when he had booked 'Braithwell Working Men's Club' with his Go-Go dancers show. Ron now describes how the evening unfolded. "I remember the club being packed to the rafters, during the evening the girls would get up on stage and dance to a couple of records every half hour or so. When the girls were in the mood they could hypnotise an audience like two snakes doing an erotic dance, but I could tell that the audience expected to see more flesh. As the evening wore on I could sense something in the air was not right so I had a word with the girls and asked them to pull off their blouses as the last record finished. My mate was to go outside and start the car when I gave him the nod. As soon as the girls had pulled their blouses off I turned the

THE ADVERTISER, SAT., AUG. 17th, 1968   21

INDECENT STRIP SHOWS RESULT IN 13 AT COURT

The Sunday strip shows at Braithwell Working Men's Club were described at the Doncaster West Riding Magistrates' Court on Tuesday as "indecent in the extreme."

Mr. Frank Taylor, prosecuting, told how barmaids left the concert room before the performances began, leaving an all-male audience of some 500 to watch the five minute strip act for which the girl performer was usually paid £10.

On five consecutive Sundays, Mr. Taylor told the court, police officers kept

Mr. Taylor said that when one of the club trustees, Frank Ackroyd, was interviewed by police he told officers "I voted against it from the start. I have no time for that sort of business. I was outvoted 12 to 1."

For the club officials, Mr J. H. Dunk said: "It is going on all over the country. It started when the club was running short of money. I do not think these particular shows have had any effect on the morals of the people who attended. There will be no further shows, and the

20

stage lights off, unplugged my decks and we all scarpered out the back door while a right commotion kicked off inside". Ron still has people coming up to him when he is in town, they either remember him from the Up N Up or the Charade's early days, some even remember him from when he used to DJ on Saturday morning's at the Charade. This was when they ran a kids disco for under fourteen year olds, from 10 am to 12 noon .

Dave Allen explained "when you have a night club that is empty you have to find ways to bring people in, so I came up with the idea of the Saturday morning club. Mums would drop their children off before going to do the shopping or have a hair do". Some Saturday mornings they would be in fancy dress and Julie Wood remembers spending all week getting her outfit ready only to be beaten by her cousin who didn't have an outfit. She explains, "My mum came up with the idea of putting a sheet over her body and tying a tie around her head, so that she could go as an Arab, what's worse is that she won the fancy dress competition". Young teenagers like Mick Holmes from Thurcroft would travel the five miles by bus on his own just to go to the club, while Terry Moore from Whiston would walk the two miles with his friends every Saturday Morning, both would eventually go to the club at night.

Most of the youngsters from the kids club would go at night as they got older, with a few actually going to work at the Charade, like Yvonne Cross nee Jackson. Yvonne remembers going with her friends the very first time when she was only twelve. "Going to a night club, even on a Saturday morning made you feel like you were grownups. We could spend all Friday at school talking about what we were going to wear the next day", she explained. Yvonne and her friends carried on going until they were fifteen, but remembers being refused entry when they tried to get in one Friday night when still only fifteen years old. Ron has fond memories of the Charade being very busy and packed to the ceiling, especially at the weekends with a great atmosphere all night long; his future wife, Ann Guy from Whiston, remembers that her parents wouldn't let her go to the Saturday morning club with her school friends, she had to wait until she was sixteen. "One of the advantages of being a DJ was that wherever you went, there would always be a job for you. So one summer I saved up all my holidays from Firth Vickers for the year and went to Scarborough, I had found myself digs for a month and got a job as the resident DJ at the Scene One night club in the resort" remembers Ron.

On the 24th of December 1968 the Charade threw its first ever Christmas Eve party. This was the same day that three Americans first orbited he moon. They were Frank Borman, James Lovell and William Anders, they orbited the moon in Apollo 8, a total of ten times before firing their rockets and heading back to earth. They were also the first people to see the other side of the moon.

The Christmas number one for this year was Lily the Pink by Scaffold, it reached the coveted number one spot on December 11th and stayed there for three weeks, but it was not a record that you would dance to. The biggest selling single of the year was Hey Jude by The Beatles selling 850,000 records in this year alone. As the swinging '60s started to draw to a close in the capital, the teenagers around South Yorkshire had finally got a night club of their own. One that would be open five nights a week, catering to all tastes in music. Dave Allen and John Stead would not make the same mistake as previous night club owners of only opening one or two nights a week or falling foul of the local licensing authorities.

The Hague Sisters.

By 1969 the club became so popular that only four adverts appeared in the local Advertiser for this year. With no drinks licence as yet for a Sunday, Dave Allen came up with the idea of a Sunday All Day Session running from 2.30 through till 10.30pm, the first one being on the 5th May. These would later be known as All-Dayers and became popular throughout the north of England.

Kathleen Dickinson was one of the first teenage girls to go to the Charade when it was taken over by Dave Allen, this is her story,

Born in 1952 in Greasbrough Kathleen passed her 11 plus and went to the Girls High School where she meet one of her lifetime friends Veronica Hague, (her younger brother is the Foreign Secretary). It was her family who would go on to supply all of Dave Allen's night clubs in the North of England with drinks and snacks as his empire expanded over the next ten years. Along with her other two friends Ann and Denise they would meet at Veronica's before going out, as Kathleen remembers "we'd all meet up at their house and I'll never forget seeing their house full of bottles of pop and bags of crisps everywhere. To all of us it was a treat at weekends to have crisps or pop, because there was no money around. We'd then catch the 7.15 pm bus into town and go to the Pendulum club; I knew one of the DJ's Dinky Dawson, because he went to school with my older brothers. To us it was great being able to go into a night club and if you were asked to dance on stage, you thought you were someone special for weeks". Living in Greasbrough Kathleen would often see the world famous stars going into Greasbrough Club, with her friends she would stand outside the stage door to see Jayne Mansfield, Dicky Valentine and Peter and Gordon to name a few .

One day Kathleen and her friends decide to go to Sheffield as she explains "we were only fourteen at the time and heard about this group called Geno Washington and his Ram Jam Band appearing at the Mojo. Well we thought we'll get dressed up and sweet talk our way into the club if they refuse us entry, which the bouncer did. So we told him how we were fans of his and had travelled all the way from Greasbrough by bus, we really laid it on thick, so he let us in, on the understanding that we stood near him all night long, which we didn't when he got busy. By the time he came on we were at the front of the stage star struck, it was the first live act any of us had seen, and then the bouncer saw us and made us come to the back, but as soon as he was busy we'd moved to the front again".

Back in town at the Pendulum and the LBJ club the three lads around town were Vic Chambers, Morris Roland and Ron Hull. "If they even looked at you, you where star struck, we'd be saying he's just looked at me, but they were older than us and soon moved onto other clubs", as Kath remembers. One of Kath's older brothers was a chef at the Brecon Hotel; this was where Lulu, Jayne Mansfield, Vince Hill etc would stay when in the area.

Vince Hill became very close friends of Athel Carr who owned the Brecon, and named his first son Athel after him. Kath also remembers the kitchens at the Brecon. "Sometimes we'd all meet there, me, Sally and Veronica Hague with Liz and Janet Carr before going off to the Charade and as a treat we'd go into the kitchens just to look into the fridges full of meringue and bowls full of blackberries. I know it seems daft now but we'd never seen a meringue and if you wanted blackberries you had to go and pick them off a bush. Because money was tight as we grew up, the only way we got to taste alcohol was by raiding the drinks cabinet in our parents' houses. What we did was to pour a small amount of every opened bottle into a small bottle, then shake it up and drink it. This kept us giddy for hours".

When the Charade started the Sunday all day sessions Kath and her friends would be there until 4.30 pm as she recounts, " between 4.30 pm and 5 o'clock about 25 of us would catch a bus back into town and go to the pictures. By this time we'd started to knock around with Neil Townsend, Dave Brown who went onto marry one of my friends, Trevor Williams and Tabs Mc Kane, I still blame them for leading us astray then, Trev or Tabs would pay to go into the pictures and then open the emergency exit door to let the rest of us in. As a matter of fact we all used to take a picnic and watch the film for free before catching the 7.30 bus back home, ready for school the next day". When I asked Kath how often this happened "oh for months" she replied. Since Dave Allen and John Stead knew the Hague family, they also got to know Kath and asked her if she would like a job working on the cloakroom at their new night club called The Birdcage in Hoyland. Kath recounts "at the weekend I'd make my way to the Charade and Dave would take me and a doorman up to the Birdcage for the night. He'd either stay all night or call back for us and then drop me at my mothers on his way back to town. I also remember becoming close friends with the bar manager, who was called Pat and even went to Cornwall for my holidays with her and her family for two years". In September of 1970 Kath was 18 and left to work and live in Sheffield, training to become a nurse as she recounts, "I'd stopped coming back to town then and started to go to the Sheffield University to see live bands". Kath now works with young children but still remembers her teenage years and told me, "Sometimes I get all the young children together and teach them how to dance like we did in the sixties, with all the hand and arm movements that we did at the Pendulum".

The main DJs for 1969 were Eric Dewsnap, Ron Stanley, Ron Armstrong, Wilson Garret, Melvyn Kaye, known locally as Speedy.

Melvyn Kaye (Speedy) DJ

Speedy started working for A and S Dance Promotions in 1967 as a full time DJ after leaving school when he was sixteen years old. He describes his first time as a DJ at Swinton Comprehensive School. "When I was thirteen years old the school started a disco and since I was the only one at school with any records they naturally asked me if I would be the DJ". He goes on "I started to buy records when I was twelve years old after listening to them on Radio Luxembourg late at night using my small transistor radio, which I hid under the bed clothes. At the time I should have been getting my sleep in ready for school the next day". A and S dance promotions had, by late 1966, started running a dance at the Public Hall in Mexborough, which as a lover of music was a magnet for Speedy, like money is cocaine to a capitalist, soul music is to Speedy. He carries on explaining "I went out of my way to get to know the DJ there, who was called Wilson Garret, his real name being John Ruthven and it was through him I got to know Dave Allen and John Stead". One weekend Wilson Garret was not available "so Dave asked me if I could do it", explains Speedy "I played the records I had with me, which were mainly soul and after wards Dave came over and thanked me, so that's how I came to work for A and S".

When the Charade first opened under Dave Allen it was only natural that

Speedy and Wilson Garret would be two of the DJs to work there, Wilson's type of music was mainly pop orientated from the charts that you could dance to. Speedy became one of the resident DJs at the Charade while he was living at home in Conisbrough. His home was only a few hundred yards from Conisbrough Castle, which is the setting of Sir Walter Scott's "Ivanhoe" an historical fiction based on a Knight who once lived there. For those who have not read the book, it is about a Knight who helps the oppressed people, similar to Robin Hood. It is also credited with increasing the interest in Romanticism and Medievalism in the 19th century.

With his suit case full of records Speedy would catch the 6.30 pm Doncaster to Sheffield bus into the town centre. He would then catch the Maltby bus from the town centre, arriving at the Stag Roundabout and call in at the Stag pub for a beer, before finally going over to start work at 7.30pm. While working for A and S Promotions, Speedy along with all the other DJs was allowed to buy four records a week from the Sound of Music record shop on Bridgegate, these would then be stamped with the company logo. This was great for the Charade, in as much as it enabled the club to build up its own record collection, so that when a DJ left, which they all did eventually, the club had a record collection which it could hand on to the next, new up and coming DJ. The down side for any DJ is obvious, without a record collection he would find it hard to move to another local club and take his loyal following of teenage fans with him. Dave Allen mentioned that, "as far as competition went in those first two years, our main rival was the Up N Up because it also had a drinks licence", but this club would close in the early 1970s.

Another club that Speedy worked at was the legendary "Bin Lid" club in Dewsbury, which opened in the middle of 1968. The club was a former Rock and Roll dance hall and was located at No 9 Union Street, Dewsbury. Speedy describes the club "it was on three levels, when you first entered the club you would go down three steps into a coffee bar, if you went upstairs you entered a large dance hall with a low ceiling and no windows, with a stage at the far end. On the top floor we had the toilets and cloakrooms for the public while next to them we had a dressing room for the acts". Sadly though they did not have a drinks licence. At some of the Bin Lid all nighters, there would be live acts on, such as Joe Tex, his first UK tour, Ben E King, Ferris Wheel, (who's, lead singer was Linda Lewis), Ike and Tina Turner and Ellison's Hog Line, a local soul band. Besides the other aforementioned DJs from the Charade there was also Tony Banks. To get to Dewsbury, Speedy would have to catch a bus from Conisbrough to Barnsley which took one hour and then one to Dewsbury which took a further two and a half hours, since it stopped at every village on the way.

After working all night at the Bin Lid, the DJs from the Charade who had no transport, would usually scrounge a lift back to the Charade for the Sunday All Day Sessions to carry on working.

Speedy worked for Dave Allen for about two years, by which time he had fallen out with him over his insistence that he play more pop style music rather than mainly soul type music.

The Christmas number one for 1969 was Two Little Boys by Rolf Harris. It stayed at number one for six weeks. The biggest selling single of the year was Sugar Sugar by The Archies, who were a group of session musicians. The exact number of records it sold in this year is not available, but estimates put the figure at over 900,000 since it was number one for four weeks. It was also one of George W Bush's favourite records; it was played at Jenna Bush's wedding party in May 2008.

21st Birthday Party

Rob Marshall, who now lives in Hemsworth, but at the time lived in Conisbrough, first visited the Charade for his 21st birthday. He remembers the night vividly "we all got together and went in a mini bus so that we could all have a drink and in any case you couldn't get a bus back home unless you left before 10 o'clock and changed buses in town. I remember the club being very small, with a low ceiling and it was before the booths were built on the right hand side of the club. The club gave us two free bottles of Champagne because there were twelve of us. But what will stay with me forever is that when I was dropped off at home the lads presented me with a gold cigarette lighter that I still have to this day". To him and his friends the club was always very friendly, but very small and hot. Like most people of his age he always went into the Stag pub first for a few drinks before walking across the roundabout and into the club.

One of his fondest memories of the swinging '60s was driving over to see Ben E King at the Twisted Wheel in Manchester. He remembers that night. "When we got there it was tickets only and we only had two tickets for four of us, so we tried to sweet talk our way in by telling them how far I'd driven from Yorkshire, but it didn't work so I drove myself and one of my mates back over the Pennines to an all-nighter in Bradford. This was raided by the police at 2 o'clock in the morning, so when the police released us I had to drive back to Manchester to pick the others up, before driving back over the Pennines for the 4th time in one night". Once back in Yorkshire he found himself low on petrol, he now finishes off his story "I suddenly realised that I needed some petrol while driving down the A1 and as luck would have it for the first time in twelve hours I saw a petrol station on the A1, so naturally I did a U turn and filled up".

The Changing Music Scene and Culture

Music in the late '60s was changing and evolving as it naturally does all the time. No young teenager was going to accept "hand me down music" from an older generation, but it was also splitting into two distinct camps. One had its epicentre around pop/soul music for night clubs and the other had its epicentre around folk/ progressive rock music for open air pop concerts, which were becoming hugely popular during this period. Sometimes unpredictable events occur in society, which are best expressed by the younger generation of the day, through their music and the late '60s was such a period.

Events would happen in America that would change the music scene forever. One such event happened on the 4th April 1968. At 6pm a bullet from a Remington 760 Gamemaster riffle struck Martin Luther King, Jr, who was the leader of the African-American Civil Rights Movement and Nobel Peace Prize Laureate. He was at the Lorraine Motel in Memphis, Tennessee, supporting the striking African American sanitation workers, (bin men] who were fighting for union recognition and equal pay compared to their white counterparts. On the 3rd April he had returned to Memphis to address a meeting at the Mason Temple church. This is where he delivered the last speech of his life while a thunderstorm raged outside .His speech is known as "I've Been to the Mountain top".

His assassination sparked riots across America in over 100 cities all summer long, whenever you turned on your TV at home, you would see American cities ablaze, night after night, or bombs dropping from American B52 bombers over Vietnam.

The soul music that generations of teenagers would dance to at the Charade from 1968 to the late '70s and which Berry Gordy of Tamla Motown had christened The Voice of Young America' changed forever on this day, as did the soul music coming out of Stax and Atlantic records. Gone were the melodies of love, happiness and harmony that the song writers of these record labels had been producing from the early '60s.In its place came songs of injustice and rebellion like The Temptations LP, Cloud Nine, [listen to Ball of Confusion] as one of the artists from Stax once said, "you can't produce those songs anymore when they've assassinated Dr King". But a bigger change to dance music would take place after the riots of 1969, which we will come across later.

There would still be popular soul records that would make it into the charts.

But most of these would be re-issues from this pre 1968 period or ones that had been rediscovered by DJs on as yet an unknown underground music scene that was developing across the north of England.

Teenagers Riot

As we look closer to home in May 1968, we have to look no further than across the English Channel to the events unfolding in and around Paris. Like a lot of the unrest in 1968, it starts with young people wanting to change things for the better and where better than the University of Paris at Nanterre. Following months of conflict between students and the authorities at this prestigious university it was closed down on the 2nd May. Now the students from the Sorbonne decide to get involved and their union calls a march in protest at their fellow students being expelled from the Nanterre. 20,000 turn up, it beats going to lectures. As always happens in Paris, the police respond by charging the students and teachers with batons during as yet, this peaceful march, but while running away some of the students throw up make shift barricades, so the police respond with tear gas.

Next day high school students and young workers join the protests in ever increasing numbers.

Mainstream singers and poets join the protest after watching on TV the heavy handed tactics employed by the police against the young of the nation. Next the trade unions, who so far have not got involved, call a general 1 day strike and over a million people march through the streets of Paris.

The government now decides to back down and reopens the Sorbonne, at the same time releasing all the protestors from jail. The students declare the Sorbonne an autonomous "people's university". In the following days workers start to occupy factories throughout France, by 16 May fifty are occupied and 200,000 workers are on strike.

This snowballed to two million the following day and eventually ten million or nearly 2/3 of the workforce soon afterwards.

A general election was called for 23rd June by General de Gaulle, who now wins a resounding victory for his Gaullist party. Although May 1968 was a political failure for the young, the demonstrations had an enormous social impact. In France it is considered to have been a watershed when a conservative moral ideal shifted to a more liberal moral ideal (sexual liberation) that today better describes France.

The Rolling Stones song "Street Fighting Man" was heavily influenced by the student riots as was The Stone Roses' "Bye Bye Band Man" and also The Pretenders "When Will I See You"

Woodstock

In Britain one of the last vestiges of government control over the arts was abolished when theatre censorship came to an end on 26th September 1968; the next day the musical "Hair" opened in London. When it first opened in America on 2nd December 1967, a lot of people were angered by the scenes of nudity and drug taking as well as a strong anti-war message at the height of the Vietnam War. The musical would not have been able to be performed in Britain without the ending of the Lord Chamberlain's power of censorship dating back to 1737, which was first introduced by the then Prime Minister Sir Robert Walpole to silence shows which contained biting criticism of his government.

Before we finish with the swinging 60s, two major events occurred in America that were pivotal to the music scene for years to come, the most well known of these is Woodstock, which took place from the 15th to the 18th of August 1969, exactly one year to the day of the Charade opening its doors. On a 600 acre farm near the town of Bethel, 43 miles from the town of Woodstock in New York State. Up to 500,000 people attended the festival after it was announced that it had turned into a free festival when over 50,000 people had arrived two days early and walked through the gap where the gate was meant to be, they then camped in front of the stage. As one of the organisers later said, "How do you ask 50,000 people to leave"? One of the artists to appear was Sheffield's Joe Cocker who appeared in the town at the 21 Club on 31st July 1965. The 21 Club later became the Pendulum club where Dave Growns learnt his DJ skills, but more of him later. Another well known blues group, the Keef Hartley Band who followed Santana on stage at Woodstock, played at the Charade on Tuesday 18th February 1971. Woodstock was described as three days of sex, drugs

The advertisement reads:

The CHARADE
STAG ROUNDABOUT
ROTHERHAM
The Town's No. 1 Disco
Good Sounds. Nice People

Every Friday
PARTY NIGHT
Birthdays, hen parties, celebrations, jubilations.
Free tickets and champagne for the lucky people.
7.30 to 11.30. Licensed bars.
Admission 4/-.

Saturday
VALENTINE CARNIVAL
Hats, squeakers, screamers oops!
Buy a "Special" Charade Valentine.
7.0 p.m. to 11.30 p.m.
Licensed bars.

Sunday
SOUL MATINEE with Speedy
2.0 p.m. to 6.0 p.m.
Members 2/6; Guests 3/-.

NEXT TUESDAY
LIVE ON STAGE
THE ONE AND ONLY
KEEF HARTLEY BAND
A rare opportunity to see this show live.
7.30 p.m. to 11.30 p.m.
Licensed bars. Admission 15/-

Nearly forgot! Try the new mid-week scene. Wednesday and Thursday — both bargain nights. Soul, and now a little progressive Pop plus a dash of dancin' Blues or somethin' and rock and roll, John Fogerty of Creedence Clearwater Revival, who were the first major group to sign up for Woodstock, sums it up best when he describes the scene as he walks onto the stage at 3 am. "We were ready to rock out, we waited and waited and finally it was our turn, there were ½ million people asleep. These people were out; it was sort of like a painting of a Dante scene, just bodies from hell, all intertwined and asleep, covered with mud. And this is the moment I will never forget as long as I live, a quarter of a mile away in the darkness, on the other edge of this bowl, there was some guy flicking his Bic lighter, and in the night I hear, Don't worry about it John, we're with you. I played the rest of the show for that guy".

The Birth of Disco Music

The other and not so well known pivotal moment in musical history in 1969 started with a riot in New York, it has gone down in history as the Stonewall Riots.

Greenwich Village and Harlem had built up sizeable populations of gay and lesbian people who had started moving into the cities after the First World War. In the early hours of June 28th 1969 the New York police carried out their by now routine monthly raid on the Stonewall Night Club, which had previously been a restaurant. Like most of the clubs in and around Greenwich Village at this time they were owned and operated by the Mafia, who would pay the police protection money for advance warnings of any raids. Since the Stonewall Night Club only had a dance licence all the alcohol was kept hidden, there would be a back up supply kept in a car a few blocks away to restock after the raid. There was no running water behind the bar or a fire exit in the building, but since it was the only gay bar with a dance floor it attracted young people from the area. The dance room which held about 200 people was painted black with pulsing gel lights, which turned white when a raid was on. To gain access to the club you had to knock on a door, whereupon someone would check you out, looking through a peep hole. On the night in question the raid did not go as planned, the patrol wagon that was assigned to take the gays to the police station was late, so some of the gays were released. They then started to congregate outside the club, while those inside started to get restless and refused to show their ID cards to the police, whose natural response was to use force.

More and more people started to congregate outside the club from the surrounding area as rumours started to spread that those inside were being beaten up. When the station wagon finally arrived, the crowd which by now had grown tenfold started to try and tip it over, where upon the police had to release more of those arrested. This lead to the police vehicles being attacked and their tyres slashed. This is the pivotal moment in history when the police had to retreat from the gay community, as one police man said afterwards, "they're not supposed to fight back, they never have done before".

The police who are still in the club were trapped and decide to barricade themselves in, where upon the mob now pent up with rage and confidence decide to batter down the windows and doors. They then threw lighter fuel in which set the building on fire. The riots lasted for three to four more nights. Long-time resident and Beat Poet Allen Ginsberg stated after visiting the scene on the second evening of the riots, "Gay Power isn't that great". While walking home that evening he turned to his long time friend Lucian Triscott and said, "You know the gays there were so beautiful, they've lost that wounded look that fags all had ten years ago".

The outcome of all of this is that within a few weeks of the riots finishing the gay community had brought out their own magazines and newspapers to express their views. They also took a leaf out of the civil rights movement and organised themselves into several campaigning movements, linking up with other protest groups such as the Black Panthers. Within a few weeks of the riots finishing, the night clubs in and around Greenwich Village would be full of gay people, lesbians, black panther sympathisers and other liberated young people coming together on the dance floor, in the words of Martha Reeves of Motown fame, "this was the birth place of Disco Music" that was to sweep the world and so upset the authorities. Like all music waves, it had started as an underground music scene by young people, but it would not last forever.

Eleven Days after Woodstock had finished the Isle of Wight music festival started on the 30th August, with an estimated 250,000 people attending. The main attraction was none other than Bob Dylan who had been coaxed out of three years retirement to come over and perform. To a lot of people in the hippy/ anti Vietnam War movement he was the new Messiah.

Matchy, who we will come across later, remembers some of the mods from the

A group from Rotherham, Sheffield, Barnsley and Selby on the return trip from Blackpool Mecca. Bub is third from left on back row

FREE PASS

FOR 2 PERSONS ANY
TUESDAY

BAILEYS

BANK STREET . SHEFFIELD

CRAZY NIGHT

MEMBERSHIP REQUIRED SUNDAYS
ONLY ADMISSION IS AT THE DIS-
CRETION OF THE MANAGEMENT

CHARADE

STAG ROUNDABOUT
Telephone Rotherham 72998

Strictly Over 18's.
Fully licensed until midnight
REALLY SPECIAL

MONDAY
FREE BOOZE

BETWEEN 9 p.m. - 10 p.m.
Admission: 15p all night.
Don't be late.

INTERNATIONAL HARVESTER FOOTBALL CLUB
presents at
TIFFANY'S, ROTHERHAM
Thursday, October 25th, 8 p.m. -1.0 a.m.
Direct from the top of the hit parade — "I've Been Hurt"
GUY DARRELL
supported by Deepest Feeling
ALSO THE NEW VOYAGE AND RESIDENT DISC JOCKEY
Advance tickets 85p, now on sale at Woodcock Travel, Church
Street, Rotherham. Late Bar

Mods and skinheads in Skegness in the early seventies

32

Mopsey with a group from the Charade in The Torch

FRIENDSHIP HOUSE
YOUTH CLUB
Ship Hill
Rotherham
TELEPHONE: 2728

...SHIP CARD

Please accept
this invitation to be my personal guest at

THE CHARADE

THURSDAY 10th JULY 1975 → 8pm
on the occasion of my 21st Birthday Party

John Rose

The management reserve the right to refuse admission
Please produce this invitation at the door

Charity Soul Night
In Memory of Judy Oates
All proceeds to Yorkshire Cancer Research
To Be Held At:
Herringthorpe Leisure Centre Rotherham
Friday 1st Nov 1991
7.00 p.m. - Late *(Please Arrive Early!)*
Absolutely No Admission After 10.00 p.m.
Ticket £3.00
Motown - Okeh - Stax - Atlantic - RIC-TIC

THE
CHARADE

Stag Roundabout, Rotherham
Tel. 72942

The Town's premier
night spot.
NOW fully licensed
till MIDNIGHT.

Smooth—Plush—Sophisticated
Definitely the Number One Scene for
fashionable people

Exciting lighting—Superb cuisine (try
our luscious steaks)—fabulous sound

Monday — Admission 15p
Wednesday — Admission 15p
Friday — Admission 25p
Saturday — Admission 30p
Sunday — Members 15p Guests 20p

STRICTLY OVER 18s
NO MEMBERSHIP REQUIRED

Available for private functions
every Tuesday

The Charade crowd on a Bank Holiday in Scarborough

Charade going down to see Dylan on their scooters and it is one of his lifetime regrets that he did not go with them. It is often stated that a lot of British groups turned down Woodstock because they wanted to see Dylan perform at the Isle of Wight; but somehow Joe Cocker managed to fly back from Woodstock and also perform at the Isle of Wight; "well money is money to a Yorkshire man". To Bob Dylan, who lived so near Woodstock, it was described "as being in his back yard", left America the day it started and came over by boat. He was then and still is today, considered by many people, as America's greatest living poet. Earlier in the year on the 3rd of July Brian Jones, a founding member of The Rolling Stones was found dead in his luxury swimming pool. The Coroner's report stated. "Death by misadventure".

The most bizarre event of the year involved football, after inflamed rioting took place on 26th June 1969 during the second qualifying round of the 1970 World Cup, the El Salvadorian army invaded its smaller neighbour, Honduras. It is known as the Soccer War or 100 Hours War. Peace descended on this part of Latin America after The Organisation of American States negotiated a ceasefire four days later.

Although the ends of the '60s were turbulent times for society (adults), for teenagers it was all about enjoying yourself. The English poet Rupert Brooke once said "there are only three things in the world, one is to read poetry, another is to write poetry and the best of all is to live poetry", but for teenagers from the late 1950's onwards it would read, one is to listen to music, another is to dance to music and the best one of all is to live for music, one such young teenager was Rita Mullet (Dramell) who came from Swinton.

Rita Mullet

Born in 1954 Rita, along with her older sister and school friends from Swinton Comprehensive School would regularly go to the Heartbeat in Sheffield on Sunday afternoons, they would all have to catch two buses. Like a lot of teenagers of her generation by the age of fifteen, Rita along with her friends, who had all started work by now, would go to The Boardwalk and Assembly Rooms in the town centre, which was predominantly for anyone under 18. At the end of 1969 Rita and her friends decided to pay a visit to the Charade; she describes walking up those dark and narrow stairs. "It was the first proper night club that any of us had been in, all the other clubs seemed like large rooms or were just youth clubs; but this was different, they had proper bouncers wearing black suits and Dickybows while inside they had mirrors next to the dance floor, with stools at the bar. It was the first bar selling alcohol any of us had seen, it made us

Rita Mullet (third from left) in Rotherham town centre

all feel like we were proper grownups".

Kev Briscoe also remembers the mirrors next to the dance floor the first time he went as well "I had heard about the club for years while still going to Wingfield School Youth Club and how small it was inside, but when I was on the dance floor it looked a lot bigger, until I realised that I was looking at myself in the mirrors". At first Rita had to catch a bus just after 7 o'clock arriving at the Charade around eightish and then leave at 9.45pm to arrive back at home at 10.45pm. Although her future husband Dave Mullet was a regular at the club, Rita explains "while I was leaving the club to catch the bus home he was arriving with his friend Des Pejko, so I never saw him in the Charade". Des lived in the town centre and went to St Bernard's Catholic School, which was only 500yds from the Charade, at the age of fourteen he was 6ft 4inches tall and played basketball for England.

It was in the Charade that he first met Dave; they are still close friends today, over 40 years later. At the tender age of fourteen he was taken to the Mojo by some older lads from school to see Little Stevie Wonder in 1967 and it was this moment that gave him his love of Soul music. Another popular club that he frequented in the town was the Pendulum club on Moorgate. He remembers the club being raided by the police, (apparently this event was quite regular) for overcrowding, due mainly to the fact that there weren't many clubs for under18's to go to, which resulted in the few that opened being full. The people in power at the time spent more time and energy fighting against teenage culture, instead of working with it. Des recalls "in the Charade I used to like the first half hour or so after opening because the DJ played less mainstream records or played the latest release and observed the dancers reactions".

Dave Seville of McCluskey's Apocalypse

Near the end of 1969 the Charade started a Tuesday night Blues club and one of the first groups to appear was McCluskey's Apocalypse, from Sheffield. The group consisted of Dave Seville, Ray Higgins and Mick Wilson. Dave Seville, who was the drummer, can remember playing at the Charade twice, the first gig being on the 16th December, with the second on the 10th February 1970. He now describes over 40 years later the group's involvement with Dave Allen. "We all found him an enthusiastic guy with a great ear for music, open and up front which was different to a lot of other promoters we had worked with. He genuinely tried to help and promote us but found it very difficult due to our unique style of music". He now goes on to describes the gigs in the Charade;

Letter that appeared in Blues & Soul magazine

"with our roadies we had to carry all our equipment up two flights of narrow stairs and once in the club I found the low ceiling a problem, because my drum sticks kept hitting the ceiling. On both occasions the club was packed with a very appreciative audience who were musically broad minded considering it was a club that was orientated towards soul music at the time. The DJ played 'Papa was a Rolling Stone', six times before we came on one night? I also remember it being very hot and sweaty with condensation constantly dripping onto my drum set". They were one of the most popular bands in Sheffield at the time, often playing to audiences of over 300 every week, at the Broadfield pub on Abbeydale Road in Sheffield. Their music was all original, written by Wilson, who was influenced by the Who, Ravi Shankar and Hendrix. While on stage they would often go off on a tangent, which was always great to see live, but the drawback was that no one could actually describe their style of music, since it was so original/underground. All the well known promoters at the time including "Tony Stratton Smith" the manager of Genesis came to hear them play, but even he could not categorise them.

Dave Seville encapsulates a teenager in a large city, growing up in the swinging '60s and into the late '70s. This is his story. Born in 1950 he describes how he came upon his love of music. "When I was about eleven years old my attractive fourteen year old sister would have boyfriends calling around at our house all the time. They where about 17 or 18 years old and would bring along LP's from America to impress her with. These LP were mainly Chicago Blues Music by such artists as Muddy Waters, Howlin Wolf, Little Walter and Sonny Boy Williamson to name but a few. Since our parents were great lovers of Swing Music (dad played the piano) it was only natural that for my thirteenth birthday they got me a set of drums. They were second hand Broadway Drums from Bitter Suite drummer Steve Bubbles Mitchell, since his parents had bought him a brand new set of Premier Drums on the 'Never Never'.

At school everyone wanted to be in a band, it was like our iPhone or Play station for the kids of today and by the time I was fifteen, I was in my third group. I'd been head hunted by three other school friends to form Delroys Soul Federation in 1965 playing mainly Otis Redding, Wilson Pickett and Motown cover versions. We were probably Yorkshires first home grown Soul Group. Our lead singer was a West Indian called Delroy who was about three years older than us. Most of our gigs in '65 and '66 where at youth clubs, but we also managed to play at the Esquire and were the support for the Clayton Squares when they appeared at The Mojo in '66.

After 18 months our group split so I joined C.G Morris Reaction Soul Band, it was with this group that in 1967 I found myself playing at The Twisted Wheel in Manchester at one of their all-nighters. A few months later I left because they wanted to turn professional, which they eventually did and at the time this meant working abroad, mainly on the American Bases in Germany; it was the pro's bread and butter". Their claim to fame was that one of the group went onto bigger things, he is Sheffields Paul Carrack, who needs no introduction here. Dave took his musical career in another direction when he helped form McCluskey's Apocalypse eventually playing in front of 2000 people at the free concerts in Weston Park near the University. These events were organised by Glyn Senior a well known local mover and shaker in the city. As Dave explains, "how he managed to persuade Sheffield Council to sponsor free concerts at Weston Park will always be a mystery to me, since the council at the time were known for being very reactionary." He now tells us how he came to be playing with a band called Redhead Yorke at one such free concert in the early 70's "I stood in for their drummer who couldn't make it up from Brighton; we all had our gear plugged into one 240 volt cable coming out of the Museum in the park, it looked like a daisy chain with cables running everywhere. As we were warming up, out pops Dinky Dawson from behind the stage pulling by its neck a 1959 Gibson Flametop Les Paul guitar out of its case and stood beside him in a very fetching white dress over his blue jeans was Peter Green of Fleetwod Mac fame.For the next 20 minutes he did an impromptu gig with us, we just followed each other musically using a lot of eye contact, no doubt Dinky had pulled one out of the bag that day". This same guitar is now reputed to be worth over $2 million. During the early '70s besides playing the Universities circuit, McCluskey's worked alongside Sheffield Theatres and the Crucible. This was due mainly to the influence of Mick Wilson, but by the mid '70s with still no record deal in sight the band split up. Mick Wilson went onto York University in 1976 and after six years left with a BA Hons Music 1st class, PhD in Composition, and is now a Senior Lecturer in music at Salford University. He is also a renowned composer of classical pieces, a sculptor and painter. Ray Higgins stayed in the building trade in Sheffield concentrating on attic conversions while Dave Seville also went onto university in 1978 and came out with a 1st in English Literature and a Masters Degree in Drama and Politics, he then became a teacher rising to become Head of the English Department. He now performs in a group called the Hummingbirds; the music they play is Chicago Blues and that takes us full circle to where he started.

Chapter 2

Neil Saint John (Noddy) DJ

In early 1970 a new DJ entered the Charade's history, but he became no ordinary DJ, as different types of music ebbed and flowed across the Atlantic, he rode the waves of soul music like a surfer. But the type of soul music and its lifestyle he becomes synonymous with, would eventually come crashing down upon him, leaving him washed ashore on a lonely island.

He is known as "Noddy", or "Neil St John", but his real name is Neil Thickett. He was born in 1953 and went to Maltby Grammar school while still living in Swinton. He has fond memories of going to the Detroit Wheel (Ron Stanley) at the Brecks community centre when only fifteen years old. In his own words, "hundreds used to go; it was a great place for music but closed after a few weeks".

He now tells his story, "When I was sixteen and doing my "O" levels at school I bought myself a scooter, but to pay for it I had to get a weekend job. So I started working as a trainee butcher at Fine Fare supermarket under the Charade on a Friday evening, four 'til eight and also Saturday afternoons. My first job was to pack up cuts of fresh meat onto trays, which we then placed onto the shelves, this involved sealing the bags of meat with hot wire; I can still remember the smell of burning meat over 40 years later. As soon as I had finished work I would go straight into the Charade, which was only upstairs.

On the night that changed my life forever, I wandered over to the top of the stairs to get some fresh air and started talking to Dave Allen, "Dave asked me if I was enjoying myself?", I replied "yes, but your DJ is rubbish", where upon he said to me, "do you think you can do any better then?" Naturally I said "yes". "Why not try next week," said Dave and that is how I came to work for A and S Dance Promotions. Little did I know at the time that the DJ, I was criticising was going on holiday, but Dave decided to keep this to himself. I then spent all the following week getting my records into a playing order and arrived early at the Charade on the following Friday, with two bags of records on the back of my scooter". He now describes his first ever gig, "I couldn't believe how nervous I was, it wasn't the playing of the records, but the talking over the mic that took some time to get used to. The night must have been a success because the following week I was given a mid week spot. Dave explained that he couldn't have a DJ called Neil Thickett because it doesn't sell, so he said we'll use your nickname from school". He then became one of the Charade's regular DJs, eventually working up to Friday and Saturday night sessions. He has fond memories of those early days at the club as he explains, "it was not uncommon for the amplifiers to burn out due to the insistence of us playing them at full volume, so a spare was built into the console which we could bring into life at the flick of a switch We also did the same for the microphones.

"In the summer it would get very hot due to the place being so full, the low ceiling didn't help either. There was always a strong smell of Brut aftershave wafting through the club like an invisible fog, since this was the only aftershave men would use then. Because the dance floor was sprung, it caused the record needle to jump when playing, the only way around this was to use sellotape to hold a half penny onto the record arm, until after much harassment with Dave he insulated the DJs console from the dance floor.

"I decided to leave school at seventeen while I was studying for my 'A' levels, I already had good 'O' level grades and since I was working I couldn't see the point in them. I'd also got a Saturday job, working in a betting shop as well". On Sunday nights, along with the other mods from the town he would go to Clifton Hall. He describes those nights "all the mods would be dancing to the soul music while the squares as we called them, would gather on the balconies and throw pennies at us. On some nights the best dancers, who we all admired , would get up on the stage and dance before the hundreds of people in the Hall; it was not unknown for one of them to put a table on the stage and proceed to dance on the top of it".

Noddy worked from the age of sixteen until he was 23 for A and S, running

Noddy with a girl in the South of France in the early 1970s

40

two record shops in Chesterfield and Buxton. He also lived above the record shop in Chesterfield while he was the DJ at the Adam and Eve night club in the town centre. One of his early finds as an avid record collector was "You're Ready Now", by Franki Valli and the Four Seasons. He discovered this with an old friend when they were allowed to go through boxes of old records at the Rediffusion shop, after it had decided to stop selling records, he found two copies.

Seeing a gap in the market to sell records to the DJs in Sheffield, he would pick ten records for his best customers and deliver them personally, as he mentions "I'd call around to wherever they were working and drop the records off with them, I'd just explain to them to give me back the ones you don't want next time and I'll only charge you for the ones you've taken". He now goes into detail why "the advantage for me was that I was getting into all the clubs for free, especially the Fiesta which had just opened, so I would walk back stage and see all the great acts preparing to go on, usually I'd have someone along with me as well".

Now that he was a well known DJ, he started to live the life style of a growing band of DJs and club goers in an underground soul music scene that was developing across the Midlands and the North of England. Some of the night clubs he would frequent when not working are as follows, the Mojo in Sheffield, the Attic in Doncaster, The Broken Wheel, in Retford, the Normanton all-nighters, The Torch all-nighters in Stoke on Trent and the Bin Lid in Dewsbury. Eventually the wave he had been surfing for the last six to seven years came crashing down upon him, in the words of the great English poet William Blake "The road to excess leads to the palace of wisdom... for we never know what is enough until we know what is more than enough"

The name Neil St John was given to him by Dave Allen, who explained to him one day, "I can't have someone running my record shops and being a DJ called Noddy; it's not professional enough, so we'll have to change your name. There's a well known footballer called Ian St John, so how do you like Neil St John". Neil now goes into more detail "it was a nightmare having three names, with people ringing up and asking for Noddy, then someone asking for Neil St John, and the final straw was that all the record shop bank accounts were in my real name, Neil Thicket, so in the end I changed my name by deed poll to Neil St John".

In June of that year we see for the first time, an advert for the Charade with the admission price in the new currency of decimalisation, 10 New Pence on a Wednesday night; this was the equivalent of two shillings in the old money. The pound went from 240 pence to the pound to 100 new pence to the pound. This was also the year that Pat Sweetwater, a former DJ for Pete Stringfellow at the Penthouse and Broadway night clubs in Sheffield, came to work at the Charade. In October we see the new look logo for the Charade for the first time in the Advertiser, of a woman's face; this logo was used until the middle of 1975

Christine Rogers, Queen of the cloakroom

Christine describes her involvement with the Charade, "I first started to go to the Sunday afternoon sessions and I can remember we had to queue for nearly half an hour to get in since it was that popular. Because I was doing my 'A' levels my parents wouldn't let me go at night, so when they went out on Friday nights I'd dash up stairs and get changed. It was also my job to baby sit my two younger brothers, so we had a deal, they kept quiet about me and I wouldn't make them have a bath. About ten o'clock I'd rush home, get changed again and wet the bath room floor and the bottom of their hair to make it look like they'd had a bath. Eventually I got a job on the cloakroom in the summer holidays, which was OK with mum and dad. One night we were given some tickets to hand out for one of the clubs private parties, so naturally me and Angela gave the tickets to two lads we fancied, Angela's lasted two weeks, mine lasted 40 years, we're still happily married.

Tucked in that little cloakroom with a full view of the club we both felt like queens of all we surveyed. When I was eighteen I went to Nottingham Poly to train as a teacher and by the time I came back, both my younger brothers had started to go to the club and I wasn't going into a night club where they went, so that is the end of my story".

Mick Dailing would also meet his partner for life at the Charade as he explains "I used to go to the Co-op with lads from college, Howard Coffey and Sid. One night I couldn't get in the Co-op, but the others did, so I walked up to the road and followed some guys in front who I saw go into the Charade. At that time I didn't even know there was a club there since I lived the other side of the Co-op and never came this far up. As I was walking up those narrow stairs behind some women I thought, she's nice and what made her stand out is that she was wearing similar style clothes to me. Straight away I knew we had something in common. Inside the club the music just blew me away and I remember standing there all night just listening to the music and not knowing anyone. Within a few weeks I got to know Carol Maude and made a whole lot of new friends there that I still knock around with, Paul Timmis and Chris Mears to name a couple". In 1975 he married Carol Maude and they are still together, the style of clothes that they had on that night where Ben Sherman shirts with Two Tone jacket and trousers for Mick with Carol wearing Two Tone skirt and jacket. After one night in the Charade, Carol was rushed into Hospital with appendicitis and while she lay in bed her only thought was "I hope my young sister is not wearing my Sheepskin coat".

The Blues Nights, courtesy of Terry Swift DJ

Alongside Soul, Motown and Pop music at the weekends Dave Allen saw an opportunity in the market for a midweek blues night at the Charade, he was well aware of the Woodstock phenomena in the music scene. Terry Swift now takes up the story "At the time I was working for Series Sound as a roadie most weekends and on my nights off I would frequent the Charade. One night I got talking to Dave and put a proposition to him, to have a mid week Blues Night with live bands on and myself playing Blues/ Progressive Rock Music the other nights. Looking back on it now, it seems to me that we were on the same wave length at the time".

It is Terry Swift whom we all have to thank for making those 'Tuesday Blues Nights' a great success. Like all other DJs at the Charade he was given an account at the Sound of Music, where-upon over the next couple of years he built up a great LP record collection for the club. With his contacts and friends at Sheffield University the Charade started to advertise the 'Blues Nights' in the Sheffield Star thereby spreading the word around the region. Terry now explains those legendary nights; "The buzz around the music scene when we had Keef Hartley Band on was tremendous, especially when you realise that six months earlier they had appeared at Woodstock in front of 500,000 hippies" following the blistering session by Santana. In their own words, "we had our own set list sorted before going on stage and started with a slow number and it went downhill from there". Terry carries on his story "a large contingent had come from the university, as well as all the progressive/ blues lovers

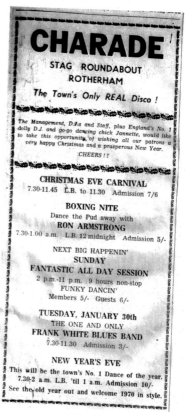

CHARADE

STAG ROUNDABOUT
ROTHERHAM

The Town's Only REAL Disco !

The Management, DJs and Staff, plus England's No. 1 dolly D.J. and go-go dancing chick Jannette, would like to take this opportunity of wishing all our patrons a very happy Christmas and a prosperous New Year.
CHEERS ! !

CHRISTMAS EVE CARNIVAL
7.30-11.45 L.B. to 11.30 Admission 7/6

BOXING NITE
Dance the Pud away with
RON ARMSTRONG
7.30-1.00 a.m. L.B. 12 midnight Admission 5/-

NEXT BIG HAPPENIN'
SUNDAY
FANTASTIC ALL DAY SESSION
2 p.m.-11 p.m. 9 hours non-stop
FUNKY DANCIN'
Members 5/- Guests 6/-

TUESDAY, JANUARY 30th
THE ONE AND ONLY
FRANK WHITE BLUES BAND
7.30-11.30 Admission 3/-

NEW YEAR'S EVE
This will be the town's No. 1 Dance of the year.
7.30-2 a.m. L.B. 'til 1 a.m. Admission 10/.
See the old year out and welcome 1970 in style.

from around the area, I remember the band complaining on the night that there was nowhere to rehearse, so we let them use the back office and when I walked in to the office, it was like a scene from Woodstock, but only in miniature.

The band went down well with their unique style of folk, blues music, but I know that some of the audience were expecting more of a rock performance". He now describes the scene inside when no bands were on. "When I first started the Tuesday Blues Club, people would mainly come just to sit and listen to the LP's they'd either sit around in groups on the dance floor or in the booths, it made a change to listen to LP's and not be on your own, like at home. Quite a few of the regulars would bring along their own LP's for me to play; I'd usually end up playing the entire LP". Some of the groups that appeared on Tuesday nights in 1970 besides McCluskeys Apocalypse (they appeared twice, once in '69 and once in 1970) are as follows, The Emotion; Junior's Eyes; Weeping Sack- who were a local band from Dinnington; Shape of the Rain from Chesterfield; The Strawbs who appeared on 21st April with Rick Wakeman on keyboard, (he left the group in 1971 to join the progressive rock band 'Yes'). He is also known for playing on tracks by Cat Stevens (Morning has Broken) and David Bowie (Life on Mars and Changes) plus numerous other artists of the time. The most expensive Band to appear there was the Keef Hartley Band, who performed on the 18th February 1970, the admission price being fifteen shillings. It would be only six shillings for the Strawbs. Regular admission prices at the weekend then was four or five shillings. On most Blues nights Tim Stevenson, a future DJ at the Charade and Co-op would also be in the club, but sadly he could not afford the fifteen shillings to see Keef Hartley. For the same money in February you would have

44

been able to see Booker T. and the M.G's with Blue Mink and Jimmy Ruffin at the City Hall in Sheffield.

Tim explained that one of the best acts he ever saw at the Charade was Frank White from Sheffield.

He clearly remembers seeing him on stage dressed in a white shirt, black jeans and waistcoat, battered black Cuban heeled boots and to finish it all off, a black hat. In Tim's words "he looked like a rock star". Terry picks up his story again "as the progressive rock movement was taking off the atmosphere on Tuesday nights started to change with the punters wanting me to play more rock music to dance to, with less emphasis on blues and folk music, at the same time the groups were demanding more money, so we had to drop the live bands which in turn had the effect of less people coming.

After about 18 months I turned up one Tuesday night to find the doors locked. The previous week Dave had asked for all the LP's back. I tried to argue and offered to buy some for a few quid, but he was a cute business man and was having none of it. He then pulled out a list from the Sound of Music with them all on. By this time we were only getting 80 regulars in, so ended my days as a DJ, with no records to show for it, only great memories and my favourite group that I was the compere for being Weeping Sack".

Terry was born in 1951 and went to Kimberworth School, which he left when he was fifteen. In his words, "I got myself an apprenticeship at a steel firm where Meadowhall is now; it was the guys from there that first took me to the Mojo, but being only fifteen I always felt uneasy there". He mentions a couple of groups who he saw perform there "I saw one group who were billed as the Four Tops, but I don't think they were the Four Tops and another group calling themselves the Temptations, but I don't think they were either". He now describes his favourite club in the town "for me my favourite club was the Pendulum. It looked so sophisticated to a fifteen year old and was always packed to the ceiling; I was even there one night when the police raided it for being over crowded". After the Blues Nights he packed up being a DJ, "I was always late at work in the morning; they even had me in the office to warn me about my time keeping. Sometimes I'd roll in at 3am after Dave had given me a lift home via the services down the M1 for some food. We'd talk mainly about the music scene and how it was changing; in those days even though we weren't cosmopolitan we had a great Live Band music scene". This then moved onto the Co-op after the Charade had finished their 'Tuesday Blues Nights'.

1970 was also the year of the third and the last Isle of Wight musical festival, with the crowds estimated at between six and seven hundred thousand people on an island with a population of 100,000 people. The star attraction was Jimi

Terry Swift, Blues DJ

Hendrix and the festival ran for four days from 26th to 31st of August. Because of the large numbers of hippies on the island for the festival and the opposition from the vocal residents, who were mainly elderly people who had gone to the island to retire, plus the bad planning of the organisers, an Act of Parliament, named Isle of Wight County Council Act 1971 was rushed through Parliament. This clearly stated that any event where more than 4,999 people would be expected would need a license from the local council. Parliament had in effect killed off the growing pop music festival movement.

Within a few weeks of headlining the Isle of Wight festival Jimi Hendrix was found dead in his bed at the Samarkand Hotel at 22 Lansdowne Crescent, Notting Hill in London on the 18th of September, his death was declared an open verdict by the Coroner. His last public performance was at Ronnie Scott's club in London with the American band 'War'; His most famous and early recordings were on the Reprise record label that was set up by Frank Sinatra in 1960, Sinatra set up this recording label with its founding principal, "To give all artists more artistic freedom". Hendrix is buried at Renton in Washington. He is credited as being the greatest Electric Rock Guitarist of all time.

Dave Growns DJ and Manager

Dave Growns became a DJ at the Charade in August 1971; he had previously stood in one night to help out when the resident DJ was ill. "I remember Dave Allen coming over to me at the end of the night and thanking me for helping them out; to my surprise he offered me a job there and then. This was the start of my long time career with A and S Dance Promotions". This is his story,

Born in 1944 in Eastwood his parents moved to Broom Lane in 1953, in 1956 he passed his eleven plus and attended the local Grammar School, leaving in 1961 to work at 'Allianz Insurance' in Sheffield. He now explains those early days as a DJ. "In 1963 myself and Arthur Clover started to DJ at the Walkers Dance Studio, which was near the old football ground called Millmoor. Our next job was at Broom Methodist church youth club. While there I picked up the habit of always listening to the 'B' side of the records, even in those early days I found myself looking for music that was not just mainstream.

Later on both of us moved to the 21 Club with Dinky Dawson which was run by Roger Brooks. He also wrote for the Advertiser. When he changed the name to the Pendulum Club all three of us became the resident DJs and in those early days you only had one deck for the records, so you would place seven records on top of each other and as one finished the next one would drop onto the deck to be played. The downside of this was; you always had to remember what order you had placed them in". As you read the adverts, from 1965 to the end of 1967 you will notice that the town had a vibrant club scene for 15 to 19 year olds, with new clubs opening all the time.

The "Pendulum" former 21 Club, opened on the 3rd September 1966, "The Boardwalk" opened on the 29 of April 1967, The LBJ opened on the 19th of August 1967, (it was opened by Peter Stringfellow a close friend of all three DJs), and the Up N Up opened on the 4th November 1967. The Twist Club was held at Sheffield Road Baths, it moved to Clifton Hall in October 1966 and there was also Rawmarsh Baths at the top of Rawmarsh Hill. Sadly Sheffield Road Baths along with Rawmarsh Baths and Clifton Hall have all been demolished to make way for Open Air Car Parks.

Joe Cocker appeared at the 21 club and also the Pendulum, Dave goes on to say "I can remember him appearing and looking back in my diary I noticed we paid him £12 plus a crate of Newcastle Brown". Dave also remembers the Pendulum moving to the Assembly Rooms on the 29th of April 1967. "We'd booked this band called 'The John Evans Smash Show' and because of the demand for tickets we moved to a larger venue for the night, at the time none of us realised that Ian Anderson, one of the founding members of the group, would soon change the group's name in a few weeks to Jethro Tull". They eventually went on to sell over 40 million LP's worldwide. Sadly the Assembly Rooms were demolished to make way for a shopping arcade.

Dave carries on his story "the LBJ club was a big thing for all three of us, we'd recently fallen out with Roger and wanted to run our own club, when it opened it took off like a rocket. It was packed every weekend, but we couldn't keep the momentum going because we weren't allowed to have live bands on. We were also getting a lot of grief from the police and local residents, plus the Catholic church who owned the building, so our days were numbered". He now explains his next job. "After the LBJ closed Dinky moved on to being a roadie, Arthur

Dave Growns with Charade staff

The DJs inside the Pendulum club circa 1967

Inside the Pendulum

Inside the Pendulum - notice that it's mostly women dancing

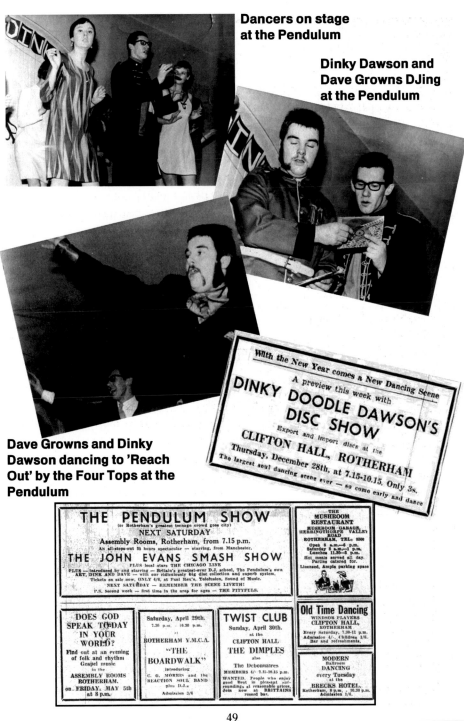

Dancers on stage at the Pendulum

Dinky Dawson and Dave Growns DJing at the Pendulum

Dave Growns and Dinky Dawson dancing to 'Reach Out' by the Four Tops at the Pendulum

moved to Australia and I moved over to the Broken Wheel in Retford for the next three years, eventually leaving after the club was acquired by new owners, who had a different music policy".

It was during these years that Dave would sometimes meet up with Pete Stringfellow. He explains "Pete would sometimes hire a couple of rooms at the Selby Fork Motel on a Saturday night and invite a crowd of us up. He'd also get a DJ in as well, so we could all enjoy ourselves, the favourite thing being the swimming pool". Dave now mentions his friendship with Pete "As DJs in the 60's we all owed a lot to Pete, since most weekends he would go down to a record shop in Soho, London and come back with boxes full of records we'd never heard of, some good, some not so good and it was these records that we played at the Pendulum and LBJ club. I can still remember him bringing back "Reach Out" by the Four Tops, weeks before it was released and allowing us to borrow it from the Mojo at the weekend, a great guy".

As Dave became the resident DJ at the weekends he now describes how he always started the evening. "For the first half hour I'd always play easy listening music by James Taylor, Carol King etc as the club was filling up. It was more background music as people milled around talking, I'd then play Soul Limbo by Booker T and the MG's quite low whilst talking over it. My signature tune was then played to let everyone know the night had started. It was always 'Who's Making Love' by Johnny Taylor, followed usually by that great dance record; 'This Old Heart of Mine' by The Isley Brothers.

As the night progressed you had to raise the atmosphere on the dance floor and hence the club, never going too high and never too low. It was as if you were controlling a wave. If it went too high it would break over itself and too low it would lose its energy. You could only raise the dancers to a high twice in one night. You would then let them down slowly to go and spend their money at the bar. As people started to drift home you could then introduce new records, to try them out on the audience. I'd start to play slower more romantic records as the night wound down, like Al Green or The Marvelettes with my last record always being 'Go Now' by the Moody Blues (this was a worldwide hit for them in 1964, it was an inventive arrangement of an obscure song by the American singer Bessie Banks).

As people were leaving the club I'd usually put on 'Soul Serenade' by Willie Mitchell". When everyone had gone home he now mentions what the staff did. "As a DJ you always finished on a high, it could take a couple of hours to unwind, especially at weekends and one way to unwind was to shoot across town to the Oasis, since they had a license 'til two am. We'd usually spend the first 20 minutes in their swimming pool before having the last couple of drinks in the bar". When the Adam and Eve opened in December 1973, the then manager of the Charade Mick Bradford, moved down to become their manager whilst Dave Growns took over the running of the Charade, besides still being the DJ with his assistant manager becoming John Rose.

A lot of the Charade crowd decamped to the Adam and Eve when it first opened, which left Dave with the task of building the numbers back up, Dave Allen had already foreseen this problem and so to prevent too large an exodus they advertised the Eve as for "The Sophisticated over 20s". In 1974 Dave took over as manager of the Adam and Eve. He later became the first manager of Dave Allen's new night club in Sheffield 'Josephine's'. After guiding Josephine's to become the premier night club in South Yorkshire he moved back into the growing A and S organisation as the Area Manager for all of their clubs, eventually becoming a Director of A and S.

When asked "what made the Charade so unique?" he replied "most of the people who went often described it as Our Little Club. It was different from all the town centre clubs in as much as everybody had been to school together, they had all grown up together and most lived within a 20 minutes' walk of the place. In effect it became to a lot of young people like a Private Members Club. It was while working at the Charade that I met my wife, Susan Mirfin who worked there with Rita Leary, Lynn Taylor (Tilly) and Angela Robinson". Below is a list of some of the staff who worked at the Charade under Dave Growns tenure.

Bar-Angela Ralton, Sandra Booker, Karen Ashforth, Mick Thackery, Lynn Flowers, Moria Nicklin, Judith Longden, Kath Law, Maxine Keyworth, Jeanette Prentice, Sue Fawcus and Lorraine Sanders.

Cashier and Cloakroom, Angela Robinson, Diane Stubbs, Yvonne Allison and Helen Addey.

Door-Ray Slater, Billy Brough, John Rose, Phil Lazenby and Steve Haydon with two dancers Virginia Shearstone and Christina.

The Centenary Pop Concert. T Rex

In August of 1971 the Charade finally got its drink license extended to midnight, it had previously been the same as all the public houses 10.30pm

The main music attraction this year is not in the night clubs, but in Clifton Park when the local council put on a Pop Concert. The star attraction was T Rex, whose lead singer and guitarist Marc Bolan, had become by then a teenage idol.

The concert was organised to celebrate the town's centenary and was the brain child of the then mayor, The Right Honourable Stan Crowther, who would later become the town's Member of Parliament.

The concert took place on the 28th of August and other artists to appear were Marmalade and Arthur Brown, Terry Reid who was billed to perform did not go on. The P.A system was manufactured by Eric Dewsnap with his partner Bill Waterhouse who were both partners in 'Series Sound', Eric explains "once we'd made all the equipment we assembled it on the playing fields at my old school Wingfield so that we could test it and iron out any faults".

Melvyn Kaye (Speedy) from the Charade is given the task of being the compere for the night, as he explained to me, "it was one of those gigs that I didn't want to do, especially since it was not my type of music, it was at the other extreme of the music spectrum". He remembers watching Marc Bolan on the electric guitar and goes on to say "I have never seen anyone better with a guitar, it was a privilege to watch and listen to him".

Terry Swift is also working that night for Series Sound as a steward alongside Mick Waterhouse, he remembers the night vividly "it was my job to carry away the young girls who were fainting at the front of the stage whenever Marc Bolan flicked a drop of sweat from his brow onto them, we would carry them around the back of the stage and hand them over to the St John's Ambulance people". He goes on to tell his other memories of the night "T Rex had been given Bill's flat as a dressing room because it was so close to the stage, yet far enough away for Rock Stars to do what Rock Stars do. Marc came out and was complaining that the flat was a hovel; much to the annoyance of Bill, all night long, a lot of people in the town looked on those flats as being Posh" remembers Terry.

When Speedy entered the flat, by this time T Rex and their entourage are there, he gets a lot of stick from the rock DJs who point out to Marc Bolan that he is just a soul DJ and to ignore him. Much to everyone's amazement Marc goes over and sits with him, they spend

The night they drove the old town wild

Summing it all up: Marc Bolan and friends . . .

the next hour talking about music, as Speedy remembers, "you couldn't wish for a nicer bloke to talk to about music".

T Rex was formed in 1967 and soon had a large following on the underground folk/rock music scene, playing mainly at student unions halls. As their music style changed over the years and became ever more commercial, their large following of older hippies in the audiences were replaced by young teenage girls. When they appeared on Top of the Pops in 1971 with Marc Bolan wearing glitter under his eyes Glam Rock was born. This resulted in all the up and coming pop groups wearing makeup. Sadly Marc Bolan died in a car crash on the 16th September 1977, (one month after Elvis), the driver of the mini car and also the mother of his son was Gloria Jones. This is the same Gloria Jones who had one of the greatest dance records of all time on the underground soul music scene in 1974.

The record is "Tainted Love" which was first released in America in 1964. It would become a worldwide hit when released as a cover version by Soft Cell in 1981. Terry picks up his story again "My last job at the concert for the night was to work the lights for 'Crazy World of Arthur Brown'. A one hit Pony with one hit song called 'Fire'. He needed as much flashing lights as possible for his act. He came on singing Fire and finished his act singing Fire, I've never known a bloke shout fire as many times as he did that night" Terry carries on "At the end of his act he would set his large hat on top of his head alight, Hence Fire".

The BBC and Pop Culture

In December 1971, Conisbroughs very own Tony Christie and the Pen Men are appearing at the Oasis night club on Wortley Road. This was another local cabaret/night club, but one with a swimming pool. It had recently opened on the opposite side of the town to the Charade. It catered for couples in their mid 20s and upwards, with cabaret most evenings except on a Sunday night when they had a very popular Disco for a few years. On September 21st 1971 The Old Grey Whistle Test is first broadcast on BBC 2; it would run for sixteen years, with its last broadcast on the 1st December 1987. It would launch the careers of countless pop groups and singers, but due to its late viewing time it always had a small following amongst teenagers.

 The BBC's first pop programme was Six-Five Special, first broadcast on 16th February 1957. It was called Six-Five Special because it went out live at five past six on a Saturday evening. It began immediately after the abolition of the Toddlers Truce, which had seen television close between 6 and 7pm so children could be put to bed. Jack Good was the original producer and had the studio space filled with the milling audience and performers, and the programme going out live.

The BBC executives originally wanted a magazine format and interfered with Good's vision by including educational and information elements which only diluted the music. This led to Good resigning in 1958 and moving over to ITV to create 'Oh Boy' as a rival going out at 6pm. This led to a decline in the viewing audiences for the BBC and since they were never keen on the show they pulled it from the schedules after 96 episodes in December 1958.

The teenagers of the swinging sixties would have to wait until the 1st January 1964 before the BBC gave them another pop programme called Top of the Pops, the first presenter Jimmy Saville claimed the BBC were lukewarm about the programmes prospect stating that "The BBC had a studio in Manchester which was a disused church and anything they didn't want in London, they slung up into this old church". This meant that for the last six years of the swinging sixties the BBC allocated only 30 minutes a week to pop music

Dave "Dinky" Dawson starts the New Year in 1972 with an impromptu visit to Greasbrough, to see his much loved mum, besides being the Road manager for the Byrds rock group, he is also one of their song writers for their latest LP, "Further On". We also receive the news that the "Series Sound" partnership is to break up, the two partners, Bill Waterhouse and Eric Dewsnap, who between them built up the largest discotheque hire organisation in the area have decided to go their own ways.

Andy Bell, Doorman

Andy Bell, who later became one of the doormen at the Charade and later Assistant Manager at The Birdcage, describes how he got his job. Andy lived at the time with his grandparents in East Dene, by the time he was sixteen he was well over 6ft tall and looked 18 years old. He would leave home at about 6.30pm and walk to the club arriving at 7'o clock to join the queue. The doors would open at 7.30pm with the queue stretching down the road and past the cleaners, in those early days if you arrived much after 7'o clock, the chances are it would be full.

Andy remembers having a few minor scuffles in those early days and after one such encounter, Dave Allen, with Mick Bradford, the clubs then manager chased them across the Stag Roundabout. Dave now shouts out "stop lads I'd like a word with you". Andy and his pals are very wary, "but we decided to stop and listen; since we didn't want to get banned", as Andy remembers. "Instead of causing us problems why don't you come and work for us instead" asks

Mick? Dave then asks him "have you got a black jacket and tie". "Yes" is Andy's reply. "Good" says Dave "you can start work on Monday night". This was the start of a long career, first as a doorman and then eventually as assistant manager at the Birdcage for A and S dance promotions.

While working at the Birdcage in Hoyland, which is an old mining community near Barnsley, Dave Allen provided him with his own flat. The Birdcage was a former swimming baths with a suspended ceiling over the dance floor and stage, one night the club was packed because 'Bitter Suite' were appearing, Andy goes on to say "We were always having to search the local idiots when coming in, we often found the odd baseball bat so sometimes we would ban them for a couple of weeks". He now describes the scene on the stage. "We'd got a full house and everybody from the local area wanted to be in the club that night. As the group started their first song the local idiot who was banned, came crashing through the false ceiling landing amongst the group and nearly ruining the night, apparently he'd found a way on to the roof and was looking for the men's toilets to get out of the false ceiling"!

On Bank Holiday weekends there would be a mass exodus to the coast, either to Skegness or Scarborough. Andy recalls one bank holiday weekend; "there was a large group of us from the Charade in the Beachcomber bar at Skegness one Saturday afternoon, when two of the lads walked into the pub wearing brand new Levi Jeans.

Not bad for free said one of them, we just walked into a busy clothes shop and tried them on and then walked out, leaving our old jeans in the changing rooms". Andy now describes what happened next. "Two policemen, each carrying a pair of old jeans walked into the pub surveying everyone in the place as they do, eventually coming over to us", "how long have you had those new jeans?" one of them asks, "Oh a couple of weeks" came back the reply "and why are you asking?". "These old jeans wouldn't happen to be yours then" said one of the officers, another cocky answer "what makes you ask that then" looking around at his mates, who now realised that the police didn't have any evidence against them. "Oh just these photos of you and your mate we've found in the back pocket of the jeans".

The Girls

October 1972 sees the Radio One Club back at Clifton Hall in the town centre, with none other than Noel Edmonds spinning the discs. The earlier start of 5 pm with the show going out live was partially responsible for a slightly lower turn out than the last time. During this period Carol Burton nee Stockdale, started to go to the Charade with her long time friend Sue Morrison nee Mills. They were both pupils at South Grove School. Over the following years it became a second home, they went that often that eventually they were given free passes. Carol was a distant relation of Dave Dinky Dawson.

On one of her visit to her auntie's cottage in Greasbrough she describes her auntie's reactions on seeing Dinky walking down the pebbled drive, wearing his full length yellow leather coat. "What on earth is that walking down our path?" She remarked. When the LBJ club opened, Dinky would sneak both of them into the club on the understanding that they stayed behind the curtain at the back of the hall all night, since they were both only thirteen at the time.

They first started going to the Charade with another school friend "Judy Oates", Sue explains. "We all loved the under fourteen club that Dave Allen had instigated when he took over the club, having somewhere to go without our parents was great", not only did this serve the local community ie Parents on a Saturday morning it also gave him "a good little earner" as Mick Bradford remembers; "Even though the kids were only in for two hours the amount of mess they made was incredible, I'd spend all afternoon cleaning it up, ready for the night".

Later this year we find the Charade along with the Birdcage and the Adam and Eve at Chesterfiled, all part of the growing A and S empire that was emerging out of the back offices of the Charade being used by a growing number of teenagers to practice their dancing technique for the 1973 Torch 'All England Dancing Competition'. The Charade with its sprung tongue and groove dance floor was ideal, especially if you knew the DJ and could get in early to practice.

No such luck for Bernie Byczkowski, Carol, Sue and Judy remember calling at Roy Charlesworth and Emma's flat that they shared together.

Carol picks up the story "as we walked into the flat someone came flying out of the bathroom backwards landing on his feet, with the palms of his hands behind him breaking his fall, it was the first time any of us had seen someone do a back-drop. He completely ignored us and went straight back into the bathroom, climbed onto the rim of the bath and did it again". At the Birdcage Rita Mullet describes the scene on the dance floor from the Barnsley Dance Team "the highlight of their dance would be when they formed a close dancing circle and then all of them would do a back drop at the same time".

Back in the Charade it was Matchy as John Rose reminisces "some nights as soon as we'd opened Matchy would be on the dance floor practising while his pal Noddy was playing records I'd never heard of". But back to Sue and Carol's story. At sixteen they both had Saturday jobs. Sue was working at Riley's the coach company while Carol worked in a local shoe shop for 75 pence plus commission per day. She remembers the queer pecking order. "In those days the Saturday girls were not allowed to sell expensive shoes. We had to leave it to the floor supervisor, since they got more commission, leaving us with the cheap shoes to sell. To get home some nights we would scrounge a lift home, which meant 4 of us plus the driver in a small car. He always charged us 50 pence between us, so we christened him 'The 50 pence man', this was before we had all met our prospective husbands at the Club". On one occasion, the night before an 'O' level exam, she and her friends could be seen drinking their favourite drink, "ponies" on one of those famous ten pence Monday nights. Hangover Tuesday morning was another name for them.

Not surprisingly Carol got a better than expected grade in her exam, which was English Literature. The most memorable night for Carol, was having her wedding reception in the club. "Everybody else went up by bus from town, while I drove my car there".

Carol is like hundreds of other teenagers from around the area, who first went to the Saturday morning club, then as a regular in her teens at night, where she would meet and fall in love with her future husband, having a joint 18th birthday bash with Sue then finally having her wedding reception there. Pam Thomas also started to go to the Charade around this time as she remembers in her own words. "Whenever anyone mentions the Charade to me, it brings a big smile to my face. My first memories are of Saturday mornings when, at the age of fourteen, I used to walk down from East Herringthorpe to meet my friends. This would be around 1971-72. The music was the best I'd ever heard. I used to watch the fabulous northern soul dancers and try to copy them...never quite got past the basics though. When I was a little older (but not old enough) we started to go at night, every weekend and Wednesdays for the cheap drinks nights. I met lots of friends there, who have become life friends. Those I no longer see still bring back fond memories.

When I was seventeen, I suffered with a very bad stomach problem and had a serious operation on December 13th. As I lay recovering in hospital, all I could think of was getting well in time to go to the Charade on Christmas Eve. My friends visited regularly with exciting news about the build up to Christmas, and who would be there. Still in hospital on the 21st I got chatting to one of the young nurses and mentioned my wish for Christmas Eve, she warned me not to even think about it, but I was determined. I left hospital on the 22nd and felt very weak and spent the next couple of days begging my parents to let me go. They were reluctant but I promised I would sit down all night, and stick to fruit juice. Eventually my dad said he would take me and my friend Cath down there. I was so excited and began to get ready. Stitches still intact and plenty of padding for protection, I squeezed into the fashion of the day!

It was all worth the effort. Although I missed my dancing, I was overwhelmed by the number of people who spent time with me and wished me well, some of whom I didn't think knew I existed. There was no walk down to town along Broom Rd, waking up the neighbours with our laughter, for me that night.

I still remember it to this day and spent a few more great Christmases at the Charade".

In August of 1972 Tony Christie is live at the Oasis again, but this time the whole show is broadcast live all across Europe, courtesy of the BBC. The show went out at 11pm without a hitch.

The Children's Author. P.J. Murray, His Journey to Harlem

From the Charade dance floor to the Apollo Stage in Harlem, this is the story of Peter J. Murray. Born in 1951, Peter spent the first fourteen years of his life growing up at Kimberworth Park, one of the largest council estates in the country, before the family moved to Beaconsfield Road, about one mile from the Charade. It is while he is working at London Scandinavian as a Metallurgist, that he started to go to the Charade at the weekends with Michael Jepson and Ian Barlow. It is at a Christmas Eve party in the Top Rank Suite at Sheffield that he meets his wife Linda Needham from Sheffield.

Within a few weeks Peter along with Linda and another couple, Julie Mangham and Peter Mainwell are regulars at the Charade on Saturday nights, as Peter explains "what we liked about it was that you could dance without any hassle and we loved the music they were playing then". He explained that when he was going, "most lads didn't dance, especially early doors, since they spent most of the time at the bar or just watching, but for me it was different. Julie's boyfriend, another Peter was happy to stay at the bar, and leave me to do all the dancing, which suited me because I then had two pretty girls to dance with all night long".

As long as we can remember young women have always danced to impress young men, we only have to look at modern day "Hen nights" or go to a "Fresher's Week" at University to see who gets up to dance first and as the alcohol starts to take effect the young women throw off the constraints of their parents and society to dance as they have done for 1000's of years.

One of the first recorded accounts of this is from 2500 years ago in Aristotle's time in Greece, when young Spartan women would dance wearing short skirts, flinging their heels as high as they could to impress the young warriors. While over in democratic Athens young women could only go out with a chaperone, so they had the soles of their sandals cut to leave marks in the dirt which read "follow me or this way" and if they did not like the suitor following them they could soon rub their heals into the dirt.

Until the start of the Swinging 60's you always needed a partner to dance with, but all that changed in July 1960. It all started in a bathroom after he had taken a shower. The singer in question describes it akin to "drying your butt with a towel while grinding out a cigarette", the singer in question is "Chubby Checker" and the song is "The Twist". He has often claimed to have personally changed the way we dance to the beat of music, "any place on the planet, when someone has a song that has a beat, they're on the floor dancing apart to the beat, and before Chubby Checker, it wasn't there". He has never been properly acknowledged for his major contribution to pop culture.

The twist got adults onto the dance floor, before the twist phenomenon adults did not dance to teenage music. Later that evening he performed "The Twist" live on The Clay Cole Show, for the very first time in July 1960; the rest is pop culture history. "The Twist" was the only single to top the Billboard Hot 100 twice, in two separate chart runs. In 1964 he married Miss World 1962, Catharina Lodders from Holland.

Back to Peter, it was a long road to the Apollo in Harlem, but one that is worth telling.

Peter left school with only two GCE's and was told by his career teacher that he wasn't destined for anything other than the steel works. After getting a job at London Scandinavian, a local steel company he went back to college on day release and in the evenings,(known as Night School). He picks up his story

The Charade crowd on a Bank Holiday in Scarborough

Girls from the Charade

THE PENDULUM—MOORGATE OPENS TONIGHT
with
THE CHICAGO LINE
(South Yorkshire's Rave recording group)
Plus a new set-up, new discs, d.j.s and policy
Don't miss this great opening night and get your name on our
BEACH BOYS concert list — it's fantastic, we're not open and
we've already got an outing arranged
As the old 21 Club premises, but that's where the similarity
ends. MEMBERSHIP FREE.

TWIST CLUB
Sunday, February 12th
THE DIMPLES
also
THE ACHES
AND PAINS
Members ¼. 7.15-10.15 p.m.

Rawmarsh Baths Hall
Saturday, February 11th
7.30 to 11 midnight.
The all-American show, direct
from New York, U.S.A.
(Tamla Motown Style)
Edwin Starr
records "Headline News"
"Stand All About It" and
"Agent Double O Soul"
Plus
THE KOOL KOMBINATION
Six-piece all-coloured group

THE OMEGA MINERS
(Fantastic show group)
Plus
THE STRANGERS
Late Buses   Admission ¼.

NEW LONSDALE W.M. CLUB
WHISTON
Country and Western Night
EVERY WEDNESDAY
featuring Residents Band,
the "WESTERNAIRES TRIO"

Old Time Dancing
WINDSOR PLAYERS
CLIFTON HALL
ROTHERHAM
Every Saturday, 7.30-11 p.m.
Admission ¼, Children ¼
Bar and refreshments

PENDULUM — MOORGATE TO-NIGHT
THE PITYFULS
(Exclusively of course)

VALENTINE'S DANCE
NEW BROOM HOTEL, TUES., FEBRUARY 14th
8 p.m.-12 midnight. BAR EXTENSION
another OVER EIGHTEEN
fee personal

THE CHARADE
STAG ROUNDABOUT
ROTHERHAM
Now fully licensed till 12 midnight
★ Wining, Dining and Dancing ★
RITA
invites you to
the town's no.1 disco
THURSDAY 28 AUG 1975
The management reserve the right to refuse admission   Strictly over 18's

International Harvester Football Club presents
TOP RANK SUITE, DONCASTER
Sunday, 17th February, 1974
4.30 p.m. — 10 p.m.
ROBERT KNIGHT
"LOVE ON A MOUNTAIN TOP"
Special Guests :- THE REAL THING
Admittance on production of this ticket at
the cash desk only 50p.

THE CHARADE
STAG ROUNDABOUT
ROTHERHAM
Now fully licensed till 12 midnight
★ Wining, Dining and Dancing ★
invites you to
the town's no.1 disco
MONDAY 1975
The management reserve the right to refuse admission   Strictly over 18's

Girls at the Stag
roundabout
outside the
Charade

Rawmarsh Baths Hall
Saturday, March 26th, 7.30 p.m. to midnight
From America
WILSON PICKETT
and the STATESIDERS
(Till the Midnight Hour)
also THE STRANGERS
plus THE WEST SPENCER SOUND
Late Buses
P.S. Next week, EDEN KANE and THE DOWNBEATS
Admission 8/-

stag roundabout

NEW LOOK
Charade
rotherham

THURSDAY 2 5 NOV 19

please accept this invitation
to be the personal guest of

MART & RLR

ENGAGEMENT

The management reserve the right to refuse admission

Bob Aiden,
doorman and
DJ pictured
inside the
Charade

FRIENDSHIP HOUSE
YOUTH CLUB
Ship Hill
Rotherham
TELEPHONE: 2728

MEMBERSHIP CARD

ROTHERHAM'S ENTERTAINMENT SCENE IS ON THE
UP'N'UP
This Great New
Discotheque
at the
UD-UP DANCE HALL AND CAFE
WESTGATE
FIRST NIGHT
FRIDAY, NOVEMBER 10th, AND EVERY FRIDAY
★ Top Thirty, Etc.
★ Licensed Bar
★ Continuous Buffet
★ 8.0 p.m. - Midnight
only 3/-

Charade punters

61

"after nine years of studying I got my degree in Maths, whereupon London and Scandinavian decided to pay my salary and expenses for a year so that I could take a Masters Degree at Cambridge University in Metallurgy".

He now describes returning back to work "When I returned back to work with my Masters Degree there was no promotion on offer, just the same old job. After ten years of studying I owed it to myself to do something better. I then became a lecturer in the evenings, back at the College I had attended for nine years. I then decided to approach the Local Education Authority about becoming a Maths Teacher and at this time there was a shortage of maths teachers. After filling in four application forms for local schools, I got offered all four posts, eventually picking Aston Comprehensive".

He now tells us of his travels. "One day I saw an advert for a Maths/ Metallurgist Teacher in Dubai, so I applied and was successful in getting the job. After working there for three years we came back to the UK, my father was very ill at the time. My next job was at Grosvenor Prep School near Harrogate as Head of Science for two years. After Harrogate we moved down south to Surrey, I had secured a post at Cheam Public School which was founded in 1645, two of its former pupils were The Duke of Edinburgh and The Prince of Wales. I eventually became Head of Maths and it was while here that I took up my writing career bringing out several books under the titles Mokee Joe, Bonebreaker, Dawn Demons and several other titles".

To date he has sold 500, 000 books worldwide. His latest book was launched in New York at the Apollo in front of 2000 children. "Not bad for someone who was told when I was sixteen years old, it's the steel works for you lad", Peter reminds us. Two other teenagers who would go onto be future Mayors of Rotherham are Dave Pickering who would walk from home and Shaukat Ali who recounts catching the bus from town up to the Charade, "we all jumped on the bus and as luck would have it the bus driver was the only Asian bus driver that the Corporation had. I knew he'd tell my dad that I got off the bus outside the Stag pub and where I was going, so I jumped off, half a mile away and walked up on my own".

Long Haired Lover from Liverpool by little Jimmy Osborne was number one this Christmas, it stayed at number one for five weeks, the biggest selling record of 1972 was 'Amazing Grace' by the Royal Scots Dragoon Guards.

The All England Dancing Competition

Early in 1973 The Stomping Ground Disco opened at the Parish Hall on Moorgate, formerly the old Pendulum venue, aimed mainly at the under 18's,

Major Lance at The Torch

but after five weeks Art Disco, the people behind the venture had to call it a day after repeated vandalism and unruly behaviour by a small minority. So 200 young teenagers now had nowhere to go on a Saturday night.

We see Dinky Dawson breeze into town in July on one of his flying visits; he had just finished an all night recording session in London with Lou Reed, while at the same time helping John McLaughlin's Mahavishnu Orchestra. His wife Nancy explained that while in America, they had just completed recording the sound track for a concert in the famous Sing Sing Prison, starring Joan Baez, B B King and The Voices of East Harlem.

Late one Saturday night groups of youngsters from the Charade and The Birdcage start to head south west over the Pennines and through Buxton, their destination was The Golden Torch in Tunstall. One of the seven towns that make up the Potteries in and around Stoke-on -Trent in Staffordshire. They would be dancing until 8 o'clock on a Sunday morning, but this is no ordinary night, tonight is the All England Dancing competition. The Torch as it became known was a former cinema that had been turned into a night club. As you approached you could hear the music pulsating from the terraced houses that surrounded the club and when you entered the chemistry and atmosphere of the place hit you, for those that went, they would never forget those first few seconds.

As you entered the club, there was a balcony running full length of the club on the left hand side, this is where the bar was located. Opposite the balcony there was a stage about four feet above the dance floor and on either side of the stage there where raised seating areas with the toilets underneath. Since it had been a former cinema the ceiling was very high, but due to the club being painted mainly black you didn't notice this and when full it would hold around 800 people.

This was no ordinary night club like the one in 'Saturday Night Fever' with John Travolta, but one that would have been in "The French Connection", in Marseille, with Gene Hackman prowling around inside while outside, a Vauxhall Cresta cruised the back streets, with pill popping regulars hopping in and out of it.

It was not unusual to have DJs arriving at three or four in the morning with their entourage of young followers from their own clubs around the country. One such DJ was Allen Day and like Noddy from the Charade he was on the road to excess which would lead him to the palace of wisdom. From his elevated position on the stage he was like a shepherd watching over his flock.

When he spotted a wolf in sheep's clothing moving amongst the dancers, he would turn the lights a bit brighter to get every ones attention, then slightly lean over the stage and point at the wolves in the crowd saying "those two there are the drug squad", suddenly the drug squad would have hundreds of Gollum like eyes peering back at them, then within a flash the lights would go low as another record hit the decks. At about 7 o'clock in the morning crates, full of bottles of milk would start to appear to rehydrate the amphetamine fuelled dancers. Malcolm Heywood remembers his first visit to the club. "I'd been in about an hour when I went looking for the toilets. I looked into this room, which later I noticed were the Ladies only to see two young women jacking up with amphetamines (injecting themselves with drugs) and I thought to myself what type of a place have I come to?" When a dancer was asked one Sunday morning by a local reporter to describe the atmosphere at 4 o'clock in the morning on that dance floor", he replied "it's like spending the night with a Bond Girl, in the morning you are only left with her lipstick traces on a cigarette". This was

Detroit Emeralds at The Torch

Torch Dancing competition contestant Val Finlison

the gladiatorial, arena that Matchy, Bernie Byczkowski and other dancers from all over the country had travelled to dance in. At 3 am on a Sunday morning while the rest of the country slept the Dancing competition started.

About 30 dancers, male and female would be dancing in front of their peers, who were also the judges. After each record those with the least applause would drop out until there were only two remaining. Matchy and the local favourite Booper in the dance off. Matchy now describes the night. "I'd stopped going to All-Nighters about three months previously since I was saving up to get married. I was asked one night while I was in Nottingham, if I was going to enter the competition. At first I said no since I'd only win it and couldn't see the point in entering. After much ribbing about it I decided to enter. On the night I decided to dance clean, I wasn't having the drug squad pull me after the competition. When we got down to the last two they decided to play three more records with the audience cheering after each one. It was neck and neck into the last dance and when we'd finished the DJ pointed to Booper and a loud cheer went up from the audience, he then pointed to me; an even greater cheer went up. I'd beaten Booper from Widnes".

Matchy from the Charade had become an overnight legend, and all that practicing at the Charade had paid off. Matchy recalls that "Booper wasn't very pleased and complained to the owner, saying I'd bussed in coach loads of supporters, but I pointed out that I'd been off the scene for months and had come by car. I remember I won £ 25, which at the time was three weeks wages". "When I asked Matchy what it was like to be the best dancer that night he replied "Val Finlison from Prestwich was the best dancer, she had just won the women's dancing competition."

The Dancer's story

Born in 1951 in Parkgate, Matchy went to Ashwood Road Junior School where at the age of eleven he won the school diving competition. When he left Rawmarsh Secondary Modern School at the age of fifteen, the careers officer told him "it's the pits or the steelworks for you son", where upon he walked out of the meeting and got himself a job as an apprentice electrician in a small local firm. "The first club I used to go to was the Miners youth club in Parkgate" said Matchy "most of the lads from school went and nearly all of them were Rockers with motorbikes, but because I was so small I could only ride a Honda 50. After passing my test I realised that my feet could touch the floor when I was on a scooter so I bought a GT 200 scooter. One night I'd been out with some of the lads from college and decided to call in at the youth club on my way home. I parked my scooter around the back and when I came out it was laid on the floor with the headlight smashed and the side panels kicked in, from that day I decide never to knock around with my old school mates if that's what they would let happen to a mates scooter.

So from that day I started to hang around with the guys from college". Matchy started to hang around with the Mods from College who were Dave Griff, Yenco, Tabs McKane and Trev Williams; he now picks up his story. "When I first went to the Charade, one of the first people I recognised was Noddy since his dad had a pub in Parkgate that I used to go to. Even though he was two years younger than me, we struck up a great friendship through our love of soul music and one night he asked me if I'd like to go to the Twisted Wheel in Manchester to see Junior Walker. By this time I'd traded my scooter in for a car and the deal was that I would drive and Noddy along with Chocka and Steve Quinn would pay for my ticket and petrol.

Because Noddy was working that night at the Birdcage we didn't leave until midnight. Junior Walker was brilliant that night and it was one of those nights I'll never forget and when he had finished the club emptied a bit, so we started to dance. By this time we thought we were good dancers, we could do the 'Drifters Walk' and 'Sly and the Family Stone' which was arm over arm, but we soon found out that we weren't as good dancers as we thought. This guy came up to us and said "move out of the way I'm going to do a trick" and since it was my first time there I did as I was told. He climbed onto a ledge that was next to the dance floor and did a back drop off it. He then went straight into a spin, none of us had seen anything like it before and the rest of the night me and Noddy just stood watching him.

Back at the Charade we started to try the moves we'd seen that night, that is me, Noddy and Dave Bacon from Dinnington. It was a three way competition between us to see who could do the best moves similar to street dancers now. Because my shoe size was a size three, I could never get leather soled shoes since they all started at a size four. I would have to buy a size three shoe with a smooth a sole as possible. I'd always pick the lightest ones as well; to a dancer it's like a boxer using 6oz gloves compared to 4oz gloves. By 1970 I'd either go to the Wheel or the Blue Orchid, which was a country hotel near Draycott, which is between Derby and Nottingham.

The hotel was set in its own grounds with a swimming pool, lawns and fountains everywhere; you had to wear a suit to get in to the Friday all-nighters. It only held about 300 people and soon became a rival to the Wheel, but after a year it closed, in late 1970. One year I was on holiday with Dave Bacon walking on the beach in Newquay when Dave turned to me and said "I bet you can do a double

Dave Bacon with Matchy in Newquay circa 1972

Matchy and Bob Harris practicing backdrops outside Manchester's Twisted Wheel

Matchy and Bob Harris outside the back of Manchester's Twisted Wheel

Margret Prigmoor - Matchy's dancing partner at Sheffield's Heartbeat club

Rotherham, Sheffield, Barnsley and Selby crowd at the Catacombs in Wolverhampton

Torch DJ Alan Day (second from left on front row)

Matchy and Bob Harris practicing backdrops outside Manchester's Twisted Wheel

front spin" I said "you'll break your back trying that". "Go on try it here on the beach, you can't hurt yourself its only sand" Dave said, "so I did and it worked, "next time you're in the Wheel do it and show that Booper how to dance" said Dave. This meant doing a front drop onto your hands and instead of springing back onto your feet as we all did then, spring straight up and go straight into another front drop the other way".

Matchy now explains how they danced then "we all danced in small circles then, usually six to eight of us and someone would point to you, where upon you'd move into the circle and do a trick or two while dancing. You would then point to someone else for their turn, this way you learnt new moves and if you did anything wrong or slipped you were soon reminded about it. I even taught myself to make a slip into a dance move so that hardly anyone knew I'd slipped. If you thought you were a good dancer you'd hustle into someone else's circle and show them how it was done. I always thought Noddy was a better dancer because he was ambidextrous, which meant that the dance moves he did with one side of his body he could do with the other, whereas the rest of us couldn't. Nowadays when I'm a judge at Kev Roberts dancing competitions I always look for the dancers that are dancing to the beat of the record and not just dancing fast. When the beat is 80 miles per hour you don't dance at 90 miles per hour, it just doesn't, look right. After we'd been to the last all-nighter at the Wheel I remember we called at the Charade for the Sunday all-dayer and when I walked in they were playing some pop record so I started banging my head against the wall before leaving".

After the Wheel had closed the all-nighter crowd moved down to the Catacombs in Wolverhampton on Saturday nights as Matchy explains, "We used to meet up at the Cats, but it closed at 2 am so someone found this cafe where they were building Spaghetti Junction and we'd pay the owner £20 to use his dance floor for an all-nighter. When you walked inside the cafe, sat down one side were all these women, we'd call them ladies of the night for want of a better word, but we weren't interested in them, all we wanted to do was dance and in any case we had more than enough young women with us.

One night the guy who had the records couldn't make it so I ended up playing my records, but I only had about 40 with me. Then in walks Nicky Carter from Derby with this guy who I found out later was called Allen Day, they had the biggest box of records I'd ever seen, and Allen Day kept handing me records to play from it. After about twenty minutes I said to him "why don't you come around this side and play the records and let me go around that side, because all I want to do is dance", and that was the first all-nighter that Allen Day ever DJ'd at, "yes Matchy in a Brothel on a construction site", I replied.

Back closer to home Matchy entered another dancing competition at the Heartbeat in Sheffield; this time he did it different "I decided to enter as a couple with Margaret Prigmoor (she came from the Castleford area) SEE PHOTO, rather than on my own for a change, we ended up winning that as well and the DJ at the time was the Mighty Atom".

Twenty years later we find Matchy working at the British Library in London. "I had about 20 electricians working under me, we had won the two year contract to install automatic transfer systems for moving the millions of books they had in their archives. When you were working in the basement which was four levels underground with seven above you, you could hear the tube trains beneath you". As the job came to an end the life style of the Northern Soul scene caught up with Matchy when he went on a sabbatical. Matchy describes his attitude to life. "Life is a tramline journey to the grave yard, sometimes you've got to get off the tram".

One of the favourite dance records at the Torch was "Love Love Love" by Bobby Hebb, it was the B side to "A Satisfied Mind" which was first released in 1966. This was the follow up to his American hit single Sunny that he wrote in 1963 straight after the assassination of President J F Kennedy and the murder of his older brother Harold outside a night club in Nashville. When released as the A side in 1972 it reached number 32 on the British charts

The French/Selby Connection

In April 1973 The Torch closed its doors after only twelve months as the Country's seminal All-nighter for soul music, it later became a car park. With no weekly All-nighter to go to, the lovers of underground soul music make 'The Highland Room' at Blackpool's Mecca their new spiritual home. In the hot summer of 1973 it soon became a regular haunt on Saturday nights for soul fans from the Charade. The only similarity between the Charade and the Torch, besides the music was that young people met and fell in love there; one such lady was Susan Priestley, from Selby in North Yorkshire.

Sue now explains "for music and night life, Selby was dead, so with my friends I would travel down to Stoke on a Saturday night for the all-nighters". On one such night she meets Glyn from the Charade, within a few weeks most of the lads from the Charade have got new girlfriends from the Selby area. Sue goes on to say "with our boyfriends we would either call at the Birdcage or the Charade on the way home from the Torch, we'd leave about 9.30pm and start the long journey home by thumbing lifts, this would take us two to three hours". One year Sue and her friend Janet Lent decided to go to Newquay for their holidays but could not afford the train fare, so they sent there suit cases by train and thumbed it down, which took two days.

Sue and Glyn got married in 1975 at Selby Abbey, which was built in the year 1069. Before we leave Sue and Glyn in marriage bliss, Sue whispered something in my ear "after we'd met the crowd from the Charade and started dating them, most of us found out later that they already had girlfriends, so we christened them 'Girl Fridays' and the ones at the weekends had the best fun." This year the Charade advertises Free Booze between 9pm and 10pm on a Monday night, with admission at only fifteen pence. At Tiffany's on the 25th October we have Guy Darrel live on stage, singing "I've Been Hurt", his chart topping hit single. This was first released in 1966, but never gained much accolade or air play. It was not until 1972 when it was picked up and played by the DJs on the underground soul scene and then reissued that it became a hit

Mick Bradford, Manager

The manager at the Charade from late 1969 until he moved down to the Adam and Eve was Mick Bradford. Born in 1948 he left Old Hall School when fifteen and started work at the West Riding Motor Company as an apprentice mechanic. He describes buying his first scooter "I used to get paid £2, 12shillings and 4 pence a week, which I had to give to my mum unopened every Friday, mum would then give me back 12 shillings and 4 pence for the week. To save up for my scooter I'd finish work on a Saturday lunchtime and then go to work for another garage up the road, after two years of this I'd saved enough money for a scooter".

He now describes his Dad's reaction when he arrived home on his new scooter. "Dad used to rule us with an iron fist and had always told me I couldn't have a scooter, this caused an almighty row but as mum told him, I'd worked and saved for two years so I could do what I liked with my money".

This gave Mick great freedom as he explained "I could now go anywhere and one of the places we all went to on our scooters in those days was the Mojo in Sheffield", he remembers his dad complaining. "Why do you all have to meet at our house with those noisy scooters? Why don't you meet at someone else's for a change?" "Because I live nearest to Sheffield" Mick would reply. Mick remembers that during the swinging sixties the only place to hear records was at a club. In his words "during the sixties and early seventies there was no pop music on the radio or TV except Top of the Pops for half an hour and Radio One was restricted with Needle Time, in effect it was crap". The only radio station playing pop music in the early 60's was Radio Luxembourg which operated a

Thurcroft crowd the morning after a Wigan all-nighter

system called Payola. Only artists paying a fee would get their records heavily promoted, in steps Ronan O'Rahilly a young pop group manager. Due to the high fees demanded by Luxemburg and no air play on the BBC, Ronan bought and fitted out a ship as a floating radio station called MV Caroline. On March 28th 1964 Radio Caroline first broadcast playing nonestop popular music, the rest is Radio History. As more Pirate Radio Stations came on air and less people listened to the BBC the Mandarins at the Beeb persuaded the government to outlaw these stations by bringing out 'The Marine and Broadcasting Offences Act in 1967'. This eventually closed them all down; the upside of this was that the young record buying public would get their own radio station called Radio One.

Harold Wilson the Prime Minister described the 1960s' Britain as "burning with the white heat of technology", but the Mandarins had other plans. With the Musicians Union they came up with "Needle Time" which restricted to five hours per day the time records could be played on a radio station. This had the effect that Radio One was only part time until the '80s. When the Charade first opened under its new owner Dave Allen, as Mick explains "we'd all go up there on our scooters, outside the club would be full of scooters and in those days the roundabout was split in two so we'd also park there. After a couple of years most of us had progressed to cars, the camaraderie that you got from driving around on scooters disappeared" reminisces Mick.

When in the club one night Mick got talking to Dave Allen about work and that he was fed up where he was working, "at the end of the night Dave asked me if I'd like to come and work for him on a two month trial period, so I said yes and stayed with A and S for about five happy years".

Mick remembers new clubs opening all the time under the A and S banner with the 'Adam and Eve' opening in Leicester in 1970; this was the first purpose built club for the company, the 'Birdcage' at Hoyland, then another 'Adam and Eve' at Loughboro, followed by another one at Chesterfield with one also in Blackpool catering for the kids of rich parents. "The Bin Lid in Dewsbury we closed down after a couple of years because it was in the wrong place and had no drinks license" explained Mick. "Dave also had an eye for new clubs and would often go down to London; he'd visit the ones in the capital and bring their ideas back up north".

He now explains the new club A and S had planned for the town centre? "When the Adam and Eve opened it was stunning inside, we'd never seen a club like it before, it had a fantastic impulse lighting system over a shimmering stainless steel dance floor with a sound system second to none and the comfortable private booths were copied from London's Playboy Club".

One day while he was working at the Charade, Dave asked Mick to dispose of his Cortina 1600E as he explains "he asked me to get rid of it for him because he was buying the latest XJ6 Jaguar. I then went to Hatfield's showroom in Sheffield with him one day. When we arrived they showed him around the latest XJ6 and I remember them being very snooty with us, Dave picked the one he wanted which was red and then asked the salesman, "Before I buy it there's just one thing I need to check, can I get my racing pigeons baskets in the boot"?, "you can't be serious Mr Allen and anyway we wouldn't allow anything like that to happen in here, you do understand don't you Mr Allen" replied the sales man, Dave sent for the manager and got his way, when they saw his cheque book closing they soon changed their minds and sent the salesman to bring the baskets in".

Even though A and S had always worked alongside the police, occasionally the police had to be seen flexing their muscles, as Mick remembers "We'd always had an open door policy with the police at all the clubs and some would even come to drink in the Charade when off duty. After walking around the club one night they told me that they thought there were one or two people under age in, I explained that we didn't allow under age people in and if we thought they were, we always asked them their age". The police dug their heels in as Mick remembers "he made me empty the club and line every one up outside while they went down the line asking their age. Out of 150 they found only three" Pete Horsley was not so lucky one night "Mick Bradford was always asking me if I was eighteen whenever he was on the door, he eventually asked me to bring along my birth certificate. Since I was only seventeen I borrowed my mates, while he was looking it over some of my mates came in and all of them called me Pete, the birth certificate didn't say Pete, so back home I went".

Because the offices were at the back of the dance floor, Dave and John Stead along with Angela Russell worked in the club five days a week, Dave would turn up some days as Mick remembers ."He arrived about two or three in the afternoon and would ask one of the staff, usually me, to take the pigeons for a run down the motorway to Leicester or Derby and release them. This exercised them ready for racing, when I got back he always wanted to know the exact time of their release?" One of Mick's job as the manager sometimes was to go and drag Noddy out of bed. "At the weekends we'd be getting ready to open up with no sign of Noddy, so I'd shoot over to his flat on Rawmarsh Hill and drag him out of bed".

In September 1973 another all-nighter club opened, it is Wigan Casino and would run for eight years; the soul lovers from the Charade now leave Blackpool and head closer to home.

The Christmas number one this year "Merry Xmas Everybody" by Slade, it holds onto the number one position for five weeks and is also a million selling record. The biggest selling record of 1973 is "Tie a Yellow Ribbon Round the Ole Oak Tree" by Tony Orlando and Dawn.

Alan Fenton DJ

Alan Fenton became the resident DJ at the Charade this year, his real name is Keith Toyne. He had previously been the resident DJ at Baileys in Sheffield, his taste in music was very eclectic and in his words "if it kept the dance floor full then I would play it". When Dave Growns moved into the Adam and Eve, Alan was brought in to fill his shoes, as he explained. "Dave was a legend amongst the DJ fraternity in those days; they were big shoes to have to fill". Alan started his career in 1965, working in youth clubs throughout Sheffield while still a pupil at Firth Park Grammar School. He now goes into more detail "to improve my grammar I would recite nursery rhymes into a tape recorder and then play them back to myself". When he left school he found himself a job as a clerk at 'English Steel' so that he could carry on being a DJ at night. "At 18 I decided to get a job at the Top Rank working behind the bar, this enabled me to get to know the resident DJ called 'Steve Just', when he took a break he would let me stand in for him. Eventually I worked alongside him on the Tuesdays' 14 to 18 year old nights and also Saturday and Sunday daytime sessions. I then decided to enter a DJ competition at the Cavendish Club, later called Baileys and on the night I came second, but they still offered me a job full time.

74

When the compere asked me my name I said Keith Toyne and he said "who?". Straightaway I realised that my name was a problem, as quick as a flash I picked my friends name from work who was called Alan Fenton". While working at Baileys he remembers travelling down to London one weekend in 1970 with a local group called "Variation Show Band", to sit in at Abbey Road Studios while they recorded a song called "Get Ready for Love", they also had to change their name to "Paintbox". After the recording session was over "I left the group and went to pick up a set of Garand SP 125 twin decks that I'd had custom made by a guy in Tottenham, they were advertised in the NME and were the best decks I've ever had.

My most memorable night as a DJ was when I'd been booked to work late one night at the Selby Fork Motel on the A1 for a 1 am start, this gave me time to work at a couple of other private functions on the night arriving at my last gig just before 1am.

When I arrived I found out that the booking was for an airline company with most of the people cabin crew staff. After about an hour the dance floor was getting empty so I put on a LP and went for a walk around, when I heard voices I naturally followed my ear and turning a corner I found them all in the swimming pool naked and beckoning me in, so when in Rome". Alan worked at the Charade for two years and during his time there he trained John Parkin from Sheffield to become one of the clubs DJs, his stage name was "Bimbo" before moving down to the Adam and Eve in Rotherham. The Charade are charging only 1 penny with all drinks at half price on Monday nights but only in July, while on the 30th May, The Drifters appear at Tiffany's, the cost is 95 pence, and no cheap drinks.

With the explosion of Northern Soul into main stream music in 1974, Dave Allen soon sees an opportunity to fill the Charade on one of its quiet nights which is Thursday. This now becomes a regular feature with Noddy returning to DJ and guest appearances by DJs like John Vincent who appeared on the 7th November. "Northern Soul" was first used by Dave Godin, an avid record collector of soul music and also a writer for a magazine called "Blues and Soul".

He used the expression when record collectors from the North of England visited his record shop in London called "Soul City", in his own words he explained "I devised the name as a shorthand sales term for my staff, if you've got customers from the North, don't waste time playing them records currently in the black U S charts, just play them what they like Northern Soul".

Once the underground soul scene had exploded onto the main stream with the opening of the All-nighter in Wigan, previously unknown DJs had become overnight celebrities with their rare and very expensive record collections, they could be relied upon to pull in the crowds at the Charade. When the news papers first heard of an All-Night dance in the north of England attracting crowds of 1500, mainly teenagers, every Saturday night, they had to give it a name (catchy headlines, sell newspapers) and what better than the one Dave Godin had already given to his sales staff.

Dave Godin died in 2004 in Rotherham; he was living at the time only one mile from the Charade. It is worth remembering that clubs like The Charade were the birthplace of Northern Soul, with DJs like Dave Growns and Dinky Dawson first playing soul music in 1966 at the Pendulum club courtesy of Pete Stringfellow, while in 1968 we have Ron Stanley sending for soul records from his relations in New York. Later on we have Speedy, Noddy and Allen Fenton playing a type of dance soul music on the underground music scene in the early 70's. These DJs and their followers were laying the foundations of Northern Soul.

John Rose, Manager. 1975

This is the year that the establishment in London, namely those in the House of Lords try to curtail or close night clubs with their interpretation of the 1964 Licensing Act. It says in effect that the public cannot order their own drinks from the bar after normal licensing time, which then was 10.30pm. This meant that night clubs would have to employ extra staff to take the drinks to the drinkers, resulting in extra cost or closure.

No doubt their Lordships, sat in leather bound chairs in their private clubs, did not want to see working class people standing at bars after 10.30pm, especially when they had to be up early next day for work, to provide the wealth for their Lordships life style. Whereas in the late 60's they had used the law to close down clubs like the Mojo and other similar clubs around the country, this time they were up against large entertainment organizations, like Mecca Dance Halls and Tiffany's. Their Lordships lost, but the establishment would strike back in the mid 80's. It has gone down in history as "The Battle of Beanfield" in 1985. This was when the Charade had changed its name to The Formula One Club under its last owner Keith Wilson.

In March of this year we have a rare visit to Broom Valley School where Chris Bonington gave a lecture on the first ascent of Changabang, a 22,520ft mountain in the Himalayan Mountain Range. In October the Charade logo that has been used in the Advertiser changed to a new design.

John Rose held his 21st birthday party at the Charade this year; he remembers

John Rose and two members of the Charade staff

first going with his friends Ian Blank and Neil Leary. "We went just to listen to the music and drinking alcohol was something that never really interested us. I started as a doorman in 1972 working alongside Mick Bradford. After working all day I'd rush home for a quick meal and then go straight to my Martial Arts Club for an hour's training, after a quick shower I'd be up at the Charade working until midnight. Some nights after we'd locked up we'd drive down to the Ferrari Showroom in Derby, just to admire the cars. By the time I got home I was done in and would fall asleep in my car on the drive. The next thing I'd know is when my dad would be banging on the windscreen to wake me as he set off for work".

During this period John was working full time in the day besides working 5 nights a week as a doorman. When Dave Growns moved down to the Adam and Eve to be the new manager, much to Johns annoyance they brought in a relief manager from Chesterfield. John explains "He'd arrive about 8ish with a crowd of hangers on; they'd then spend most of the night in the back offices leaving the running of the club to me". He now recalls an unexpected visit from Dave Allen, "After he'd been in the club for about ten minutes he asked me where the relief was. I explained that he must still be in the office, so off Dave stormed to find them all having a party in his office. After the relief manager had left, Dave asked me to go and open the safe, I arrived in front of the safe and realized that I didn't have the keys, upon turning around Dave was looking at me, "Do you think you can run the club then", he asked, I'd been asking for several weeks for a chance so naturally I said yes, where upon Dave threw me the keys and said "the accountant will be here on Monday morning to show you the books" and that is how I became the manager of the Charade, a job I would do for the next seven years".

As a manager he carried on the policy of A and S Dance Promotions of letting the DJs determine the music policy, which was always at the cutting edge of the music scene. His policy of always putting the youngsters who came to the club first, gave the club its friendly atmosphere especially to newcomers. He recalls newcomers often saying "it's my first time here and I've come to meet so and so", at the end of the night the same people would come up and say "I really enjoyed myself tonight, found all your staff friendly and talkative, especially while I was waiting on my own".

To John this was praise enough. One of his many jobs as manager was to polish the beech wood dance floor twice a week, this took great skill with the electrical polisher with its two large rotating discs, on several occasions new employees would try their hand at this, only to be thrown onto their back by the polisher, with only their pride hurt. In his early days as a doorman he recounted that the club was a regular haunt for all the car dealers from South Yorkshire, "they started to arrive after 10.30 when the pubs had closed bringing along one of their mechanics, who would be driving them home."

John's philosophy to people who had had too much to drink was that they are paying our wages and it is our job to look after them, especially when they had got drunk. So rather than throw them down two flights of stairs, he had trained his doormen to have a quiet word in their ear. They would then escort them out and on some occasions, getting them a taxi for home. We also see John employ more doormen with martial arts skills, rather than just rely on size, one of these was Dave Day who started at the club in 1976 just before his 18th birthday.

Dave was from London and had a strong cockney accent, his parents had moved up north due to work commitments when he was thirteen years old and they lived on Stag Lane, just at the back of the Charade. He left school at sixteen, getting his first job at Brook Stead Panel Craft as a panel beater.

Like John his main hobby was martial arts and it is through another doorman and work college that he got to work at the club, having to supply his own monkey suit. Dave Day explains "At the weekends when the club was always full there would be two of us on the door and two more inside, one would always stand on the step near the fire exit and if any trouble started the DJ would press a bell under the record decks", as Linda Kay from Sheffield found out, she goes into great detail. "I'd always loved soul music from an early age and when I was old enough I started to go to All-Dayers in and around Sheffield, it was through one of these that I heard about a mini bus that a girl from Whiston used to put on every weekend to the all-nighters in Cleethorpes and when someone dropped out I was in", she now explains her one and only visit to the Charade " I'd asked the DJ, who by the way was Noddy, to play an instrumental called 'Lady Marmalade', he refused saying it wasn't Northern Soul and tonight he only played Northern Soul", this really got me wound up. "So after I'd talked it over with the others I went back to confront him and while I was giving him what for I was suddenly lifted off my feet by two bouncers and escorted out". Noddy had pressed the alarm bell. "When the mini bus arrived outside Cleethorpes we encountered a police road block, they wanted to search all the girls for drugs. That is me, Karen Lister, Jane Watson and Julia Wood. By this time I was fuming and I told them in no uncertain terms that we weren't going to be searched by any hairy police officers, so they sent for a woman officer who read the riot act to me". There were no drugs but on the way home she says "I got a nose bleed". The following week Linda got in touch with Blues and Soul who wrote an article about the Charade episode stating that Linda was right all along.

Back to Dave, One evening John asked Dave Day to stay on the door all night and count the people coming in with the clicker. At about 10 o'clock Dave sees John coming over to him, having noticed that there was not enough room for people to lift there drinks to their lips, "what's the clicker say" he asked, "300 I told him". Dave explains one of the major problems a full Charade meant to him, "the only way to bring barrels of beer and lager to the bar from the store room was to carry or roll them over the dance floor, to impress the women we'd carry them over their heads though. After one such evening one of my mates tried this for himself, but it was not a case of strength alone, as he tried to raise the barrel over his head he dropped it and broke his leg. Because I still had a Cockney accent a lot of the young girls would come to talk to me, just to hear my accent, much to the annoyance of the other bouncers" he recalls. Dave's wife Valery Mar also remembers the Charade in the early seventies. "We'd go most weekends, a group of us from Kimberworth Park, but it was always two buses there and two back that was the problem" by the time Dave became a doorman she'd stopped going. Dave recalls one summer, "after we'd locked the club up on Saturday nights rather than go down to the Eve in town I'd drive me and Phil Lazenby over to Scarborough arriving at 3 am, after a few hours sleep in the mini and breakfast at the Harbour Lights cafe we'd play football on the beach until the pubs opened at 12pm". He never did say whether they still had their monkey suits on or not.

Phil Lazenby, Doorman

Phil Lazenby remembers going to the Charade for the first time one Christmas when he was fifteen. "I got in alright because I was 6ft 2 inches and had gone with a group of friends called the McClares and McDonaugh's". He now tells us his story. "I started to go regularly when I was seventeen while I was an apprentice machinist in the steel works. Every year the top two apprentices would be offered the chance to train as an electrician, which I always fancied doing, one year I came second but the post was given to another lad who had come fourth because his dad was a foreman in the works".

Phil Lazenby working behind the Charade bar

So at 18 he had left the steel works to become a full time doorman, working most nights at the Charade as Phil recalls "I was one of the few doormen that didn't mind working the Monday Rock Nights, since I had always enjoyed all types of music and they were a great crowd with never any trouble from them." When I look back on those rock nights with all that cheap booze and nobody dressed up like at the weekend, I still can't believe that I never threw any of them out".

The club always made a special effort for Christmas and Halloween etc, things like dry ice and dressing the club to emphasize the special event, they even kept an old coffin in the underground car park. "One year Dave Allen picked the Charade for the Christmas party as Phil remembers; since we closed at midnight it gave us time to get the club ready after all the punters had gone home. We had people arriving up till 3.30 in the morning from Dave's clubs, all over the north of England. At the end of the night I caught the bus home at seven in the morning as the party wound down" .Like a lot of people who worked at the Charade, Phil met his wife there, June Roddis.

Saving the deposit for a home

Yvonne and Kevin Jackson both worked at the Charade for three years while they were saving up to get married, Yvonne worked mainly in the cloakroom while Kevin worked on the door. Yvonne remembers going to the Saturday morning club from the age of twelve with her school friends, until they were all fifteen, she says "it made us feel like we were grown up especially since it was a proper night club and not a youth club like the others. We'd spend all week at school talking about what we were going to wear and now when I look back on those years I realize how lucky we were to have someone like Dave Allen putting on dances for us young kids".

Yvonne now mentions trying to get in for her first time one night. "When we were all fifteen and sixteen we tried to get in one night, we'd actually stopped going for a couple of weeks hoping they'd forget what we looked like, but it didn't work". Kevin had a similar tale to tell "when I was nearly seventeen; me and my pals spent two weeks buying the latest fashion in men's suits, we all turned up wearing brand new suits but as we got to the pay booth we encountered Mick Bradford who eyed us up and down then said "You lot aren't 18 are you?" "We all answered no", "you can't come in tonight then, try in a couple of months and don't all come in new suits, just look smart". When working in the cloakroom one night, which was only 6ft by 6ft square, Yvonne explained "Within half an hour of opening all the 100 pegs were full so we shouted John over", " what shall we do now we're full up" we told him. John sent us to open the store room and put tickets on the coats, as Yvonne recounts "We then placed all the coats over the beer barrels but because the club was packed we couldn't get out and one of the bouncers kept bringing us drinks. At the end of the night we could hardly read the tickets, so we just told everyone to pick their own coat out, I was surprised that no coats were stolen that night". For Yvonne the Charade was like one big happy family, "I knew most of the crowd and the club had an atmosphere and ambience that other clubs never had for me".

SOUND OF SUCCESS

The "Sound Of Music", Howard Street, Rotherham, has been judged the best record shop in Yorkshire by "Music Week," a trade paper of the music industry.

The owners and managers of the shop, Mr. and Mrs. Cyril Charles, have won a long week-end in Nice, and will also be awarded another prize in a presentation in February.

Mrs. Muriel Charles said she believed that the competition for style and civility. The owners have run the "Sound Music" for 12 years.

MELLY MAGIC

George Melly and John Chilton's Feetwarmers (Clifton Hall, Rotherham).

After watching a series of second rate bands, Melly's slickness and the sheer professionalism were the hallmark of this show.

He's relaxed, extremely funny and when he sings he is incomparable he is the only white man around who can sing blues and sound right.

This show was a joint venture by Radio Sheffield, and the Rotherham Council and it was a sell-out with an audience of all age-groups who had come to see the master at work.

He's so unbelievably relaxed — sitting smoking on stage — have a solo when his band covered a wide spot of blues and jazz from "Boogie Woogie" to a Johnny Mercer medley. He started with a Bessie Smith number "You've Been a Good Old Wagon."

Let's have more people like this in Rotherham and concerts will be a sell-out. — C.I.

NEW LOOK

Charade

PATRONS PLEASE NOTE:—
THAT AS FROM APRIL 21st WE ARE
Extending Our Progressive Music Programme
TO INCLUDE FRIDAYS
Mondays: CHEAP DRINKS NIGHT and the Best in Heavy Sounds. Fridays: PROGRESSIVE MUSIC presented in the inimitable

CHARADE STYLE

Private Hire available — Tuesdays and Thursdays
Ring John or Bob on Rotherham 72942
SEE YOU THERE !!

Sean Hampsey DJ

1976 is also the year that the Charade's logo is changed as is the inside of the club, which is redesigned. We have Tim Stevenson as the Rock DJ on Monday nights, Wednesday nights becomes Punk Rock Nights and Sean Hampsey becomes the regular weekend DJ.

Sean went to St Bernard's School which is only 500 metres from the Charade; he was destined to be a professional musician, while still at school he was a trumpet player with the Yorkshire Youth Orchestra. This was a great honour for the school and the Head Master in particular, since Sean was the very first pupil to be accepted by this prestigious Orchestra.

While in class he was left to his own devices, which for an up and coming professional musician, meant doing nothing. Coming from a strong Irish family he recounts. "All the music at home was Irish music that my parents always listened to, I didn't realise until I was eleven that there were other types of music around".

He recounts those early days. "I'd started to collect records when I was twelve and by the time I was fifteen I'd set up a mobile Disco with my school buddy John Kennedy, it had cost us £200 to buy the equipment, we both borrowed the money from our parents, but had to pay it back over the next 18 months".

Sean's family had decided that the best way into an Orchestra for him was to join the army and then the regimental band. After a gruelling and physical two week induction course, he is accepted as a Cadet. "I still remember to this day the exact words of that Sergeant Major from 40 years ago, one of our group asked him where our first posting will be, after eight weeks of basic training, he replied "in Northern Ireland paddy bashing", where upon I stood up and walked out of that class and with it The Army",

Back at home I got a job as an apprentice brick layer with a small building company. "One day I found myself standing before John Rose and Dave Allen being interviewed for a job as a DJ. After explaining that I'd been working for the past three years as a DJ with John Kennedy, I realised that my dream of working at the Charade was slowly slipping from my grasp.

Dave Allen was asking some very searching questions about our style as DJs. He also asked us both what we did at school, "I mentioned The Yorkshire Youth Orchestra and that I was the main trumpet player, straightaway we both get offered jobs and from that day on I got on with Dave, like a house on fire".

Not only is Sean one of the DJs but when they came to refurbish the club he is drafted in to do the brick laying. Although Dave Allen along with his partner John Stead were well on their way to becoming multi millionaires with a string of night clubs and casinos across the north of England at heart they were still business men.

By now the Charade was looking dated, after being open for eight years at least six nights a week so Dave decided to give it a major refit as Sean remembers. "We'd close the club at midnight and as soon as everyone had left we'd start on the alterations, somehow Dave had drafted me in to do all the brick laying and looking back I cannot even remember if any of us got paid for the extra work we all did". John Rose remembers that hectic week, "We had to do all the alterations in the night and still be open for business the following evening". This was no quick makeover for the club but involved building a proper cool room for the beer where the offices had previously been, laying pipes to the bar area for the beer and lager, ripping out the old booths and dance floor, they then had to lay a new self levelling concrete dance floor, as John remembers. "It was touch and go with the concrete since it needed 36 hours to set, it was not until we reopened that night that we knew it had set after being down for only 24 hours".

Dave Allen had somehow got all the staff to rebuild the inside of the club for him in one week. Besides having two jobs Sean was also working for the Sound of Music's record shop at their stall in the market every Saturday.

Grand Re-Opening 24th July, the New Look Charade

In his three years as a doorman Kevin Jackson explained that it was very rare to throw some one out of the club, "John had taught us to walk up to any potential trouble makers and tell them to make that drink your last one and leave, you can then come back another night".

All the A and S management team are there for the grand reopening with complementary tickets for the other dignitaries, as expected the club is heaving with people, hot and sweaty with condensation dripping on to the DJ.

At about 10 o'clock a fight starts between two rival gangs that have somehow infiltrated themselves into the club, as it spreads like a wave onto the dance floor it crashes into the decks and causes the stylus to jump on the record, this happens to be one of Sean's rare and expensive records, "so I stopped playing the music Sean recounts, where upon John Rose fights his way through to me and says "never stop the music when there's a fight on, keep it playing". So I put on a cheap record".

Dave Allen and John Rose with the doormen try to quell the fight which is starting to get out of hand with the new brick pillars in the club falling over because the mortar hasn't fully dried. One of the gang leaders is in the men's toilet and is taking on all-comers remembers Kevin " John says, " get in there and sort him out", "so I did as I was told pulling all the on lookers out of the way. Suddenly I'm face to face with one of the gang leaders who throws a punch at me, I stepped back and grabbed his arm and using his own momentum I spun him around. Once I'd got him I pushed his head down with one hand, while using my other to grab the back of his belt and frog march him out".

When it was all over, as Kevin remembers "someone came over to me and said", "You've just ripped my suit", "you'll have to see the management about that pal" I explained. "I am the f...ing management, I'm John Stead" and stormed off. I thought to myself "I've just saved your club pal".

Tim Stevenson, DJ

Another DJ from Maltby Grammar School enters the Charades history, but he is not a DJ that is schooled in the art of dance music, the style of music that he would be playing for the next three years is Rock music on Monday nights. His name is Tim Stevenson a former DJ at the Co-op. Tim worked for Series' Sound at the Co-op under the wings of Bill Waterhouse, one of the founding members of Series Sound; as he explained". I used to help out at the Co-op and when the DJ couldn't make it one night Bill asked me to have a go and that's how I became a DJ".

Tim remembers starting the Sunday Night Rock club at the Co-op " there never was much to do on Sundays so I asked the people running the Co-op why not let me bring a few LP's for people to listen to and see how it goes. Within a few weeks we'd got quite a following with everyone just sat around listening to a full LP, sometimes we'd even have a themed night with people bringing their own LP's along to listen to. When I left school I managed to get a job in the steelworks, but I wasn't very impressed and since I'd always liked cars I applied for a job at a garage in Sheffield and somehow talked my way into the job not knowing really how cars worked".

By the time he was 19 he had passed his Hackney Cab driving test making him the youngest ever holder of this licence, his father founded A1 taxis. "In 1970 I was a regular visitor to the Charade every Tuesday night to listen to the Blues music, which sometimes went under the heading 'Progressive Blues' or 'Underground Music', but most of the time I would frequent the Co-op which played my type of music at the weekends. Since the Co-op only had a drinks license till 10.30pm, we'd drift up to the Charade about 11o'clock

84

at the weekends if we still fancied a drink. One night in 1976 I got talking to Dave Allen, looking back on it now I seem to remember that he was leading the conversation, anyway at the end of the night he'd offered me a job as their Monday Nights Rock DJ, which I accepted".

Over the next three years Tim built up a regular following of rock/blues music fans from around the area. "At first I started playing the type of music that I played at the Co-op on Sunday nights with people sitting on the dance floor or in groups but as time progressed the young punters wanted something to dance to, so I had to change my style".

Like all A and S DJs, The Adam and Eve in the town centre got priority over the Charade. To help John Rose out he would go reluctantly down there to DJ when they were short, as he explains " I hated it, it wasn't my scene at all with all this disco dance music, I didn't know what to play and had to rely on the staff there to pick all the records, to break the monotony up sometimes I'd put on a blues record just to empty the dance floor so that they could all stop dancing and have a drink, but the manager would come flying over and say "do you want to keep your job".

Tim was always trying to introduce new and fresher types of Rock music to the punters and one night he remembers". I put on a record, which was a new style of underground rock music, but a large majority of the dancers complained that they couldn't play there air guitars to it", it was "Punk Rock".

As Punk Rock broke onto the music scene in England in 1976 the Charade was at the forefront with its Wednesday Punk Rock nights.

Punk Rock is a rock music genre; it started as an underground rock movement in the early 70's around the Mercer Arts Centre in Greenwich Village, yes the same area as Disco music emerged from. By 1974 it had moved to a club in lower Manhattan called the CBGB club. Malcolm McLaren who was living at the time in New York was a regular visitor and at the time was a partner in a clothes store on The Kings Road in London selling anti-fashion clothing, renamed "Sex". When he returned to England in May 1975 he signed up a group that would become synonymous with the Charade, "The Sex Pistols".

The Sex Pistols

Carl Eggleston, started work at the Charade in 1976 as a barman while he was a trainee chef at the Art College, he worked as a barman for the next two years, but would also go on his nights off, mainly to the punk rock nights and New Wave era scene that was breaking.

Desperate to get a job and fund himself through Art College he can still vividly

THE CHARADE
STAG ROUNDABOUT
ROTHERHAM

Now fully licensed till 12 midnight
★ Wining, Dining and Dancing ★

PETE AND KAREN

*invites you to
the town's no.1 disco*
MONDAY 24 FEB 1975

Strictly over 18's

...nagement reserve the right to refuse admission

East Anglian Soul Club

3692

Official Membership Card 1976

...me JOHN KEENAN

28, STUDMORE RD

...INBROWORTH PK. ROTHERHAM

...Date of Birth 6-4-55

PALACE · MANCHESTER
General Manager : TIM H. TILLSON   Phone CENtral 0184
6.15 – THURSDAY, 23rd MARCH – 8.30
TWO PERFORMANCES ONLY
FOR ONE NIGHT ONLY

ARTHUR HOWES in association with PHIL WALDEN & STAX RECORDS present

OTIS REDDING

SPECIAL GUEST STAR

ARTHUR CONLEY

SAM and DAVE	EDDIE FLOYD

THE MAR-KEYS	COMPERE AL BELL

BOOKER T. AND THE M.G.'S
FEATURING THE FANTASTIC GUITAR OF STEVE CROPPER

PRICES: 17/6 15/- 12/6 10/6 7/6 6/-
All seats may be booked in advance

BOX OFFICE
·PALACE THEATRE
MANCHESTER
POSTAL BOOKING FORM
Thursday, 23rd March, 1967.
Otis Redding & Co.   Date

Please forward   SEATS...
for the EVENING 6.15 / 8.30 performance on
I enclose stamped addressed envelope and P...

NAME
ADDRESS
Use the form if inconvenient to call.

MEMBERSHIP CARD
2025

Charade Sunday Club

Stag Roundabout   · · ·   **Rotherham**

Member's Signature

P. Horsley

THE TALK OF THE NORTH   **SOUL CLUB**
LINCOLNSHIRE
Telephone : 05266-596 or 0522-30361

Members Name .... PETE HORSLEY

Members Signature ....

Members No. ....

...uced at all venues and is strictly

CASINO CLUB
Station Road, Wigan
Tel. Wigan 43501

JAN 7 6090

Members Name

Peter Horsley

Members Signature

P. Horsley

MEMBERS NOTE
Non-Members MUST NOT Pay for Drinks

This card must be produced by the member when entering the club and it is strictly NOT transferable.

YEAR ENDING

MEMBERS CARD No 246

This Club is promoted for the teaching and practise of all forms of Ballroom Dancing and to provide a Social Club for the accommodation of its Members of both sexes.

★

card is not transferable

THE CENTRAL SOUL CLUB

2 CENTRAL ROAD
LEEDS LS1 6DE
Telephone 33550

Valid until 31 AUG 1974

Member

P. Horsley

The Torch All-Nighter Club
Membership Card
Membership No.

No 7434

Valid until Jan 31 1973
Signature Peter Horsley

Cleethorpes
WHERE THE FAITH IS KEPT
all-nighter

Lincolnshire Soul Club
21 WEST END — WALCOTT
LINCOLN LN4 3ST
TEL. BILLINGHAY 596
STD (052—66)

Membership Card

Name
Signature J Towey

Strictly not transferable
WE ARE THE TAL... OF THE NORTH
Must be shown on entry

INTERNATIONAL SOUL CLUB
MEMBERSHIP CARD
1974
Membership Number :—

No 9086

Member's Signature P. Horsley

Charade Disco
Fully Licensed till Midnight
Monday to Saturday Inclusive

Nice Sounds, Nice People,
Great Atmosphere

STAG ROUNDABOUT,
ROTHERHAM

Telephone 72942

M C THE MECCA SOCIAL CLUB
Membership Certificate

Number 629917
Available
Members Signature Peter Horsley

Code E14
30.12.73

MB 7 Scot. Auto.

CLUB SECRETARY

BOYLAN'S, 30-32 OLD ROAD, CONISBROUGH, DONCASTER, YORKS. DN12. 3NB

THE FOLLOWING RECORDS ARE ADDITIONS TO THE AMERICAN IMPORT LIST. PLEASE ADD TWO
PENCE EACH RECORD FOR POSTAGE. PLEASE STATE AMOUNT OF MONEY ENCLOSED.

****

Just ask me (VOCAL & INSTRUMENTAL)	Lennis Guess	90p
The Right Direction	Clara Ward	90
Mighty good way	Robert Banks	90
If you ask me	Jerry Williams	90
You can come right back to me	David Ruffin	90
Music	Jeanette White	90
Working at the GO GO	Butch Baker	90
Unsatisfied	Lou Johnson	90
A Lil' loving sometime	Alexander Patton	90
There's nothing else to say	Incredibles	90
Everlasting Love	Robert Knight	85
Reach out I'll be there	Lee Moses	85
Just like Romeo & Juliet	Reflections	65
It's you that I need	Temptations	60
Space Oddity	Davud Bowie	75
Time/Prettiest Star	"	75
Twisting the night away	Rod Stewart	75
I'll say forever my love	Jimmy Ruffin	60

THE FOLLOWING RECORDS ARE ONLY 30 Pence EACH

Come on do the jerk	Miracles
Different Strokes	Syl Johnson
Charlotte	Otis Leaville
After loving you	Jean Wells
Wonderful, wonderful	The Tymes
You got to feel it	Ted Taylor
Untie Me/Disillusioned	The Tams
Standing at the crossroads of love	Supremes
Danger, heartbreak dead ahead	Marvellettes
Hey harmonica man	Stevie Wonder
Abraham, Martin and John	Miracles
Never get enough of your love	Eddie Floyd

****

Don't forget the re-issue of "REAL HUMDINGER/PLEASE LET ME IN" ...J.J. BARNES 48p
I'VE BEEN HURT...GUY DARRELL.   MONY MONY...JIMMY JAMES. . . . .48 Pence Each.

****

LATE ADDITIONS TO I PORTS

Love, love love	William Bonney	90p
I can do it	Autographs	90
Judy in disguise	Offenbach	90
More, more, more of your love	Bob Brady	90
Uptight	Stevie Wonder	90
Friday Night	Johnny Taylor	90
Angel Baby	George Carrow	90

PLEASE SEND FOR

NEW LIST 3W KS

PLEASE, ALWAYS PRINT YOUR NAME AND ADDRESS CLEARLY.

remember his interview with John Rose.

Can you work a beer pump? "Yes"

Can you count? ---------------"Yes"

Can you start tonight? -------"Yes"

"You've got the job then".

Carl vividly remembers his first visit to the Charade." While at Art College I remember going up one Christmas for a private party that the Art College had organised for us.

The students from the college used the club a lot for private parties because of their relaxed policy on our age and what we wore". On one such occasion the police came in and after looking around, as John Rose remembers, they said to him. "Some of these kids don't look old enough to be in here", John replied "Have you noticed that they aren't drinking either, we're keeping an eye on them". The police replied "at least we know where they are" and left, John had stamped his style of management onto the club, friendly, safe and relaxed.

One Punk Rock Night, Carl is working behind the bar as usual when someone unknown to the punks enters the club and goes straight over to the most attractive woman amongst them; in Carl's words "she was drop dead gorgeous but wouldn't have much to do with the young punks in the club".

On this night she stays talking with the newcomer for over 20 minutes, when suddenly she thumps him in the face, nearly flooring him, naturally he shoots off. Everyone in the club is interested in why she hit him so hard, so when she came over to the bar for a drink, I asked her "what was all that about then?" She now tells her story to him. "A few weeks ago some of us from the club went over to Doncaster to see a group called the Sex Pistols and I ended up spending the night with their lead singer and that was their Road Manager.

He told me they're on at Doncaster again tonight and he'd been sent to find this club called the Charade and bring me back to him for the night. I wasn't that bothered and told him that he could have any bird he wanted for the night from the audience, but he kept going on how special I was. So eventually I asked him what's so special about me?" "You gave him the best blow job he's ever had, that's why you're special" he said, so I hit him".

Carl remembers when working behind the bar that he could always hear what people were ordering, because the music was never too loud. This was partly due to the fact that the Chair of the licensing board Colonel Muntus, brother was living across the road from the Charade.

John Rose picks up the story. "When it was hot and stuffy in the summer the only way to get any fresh air in was to open the fire escape that led onto the flat roof because the windows at the front of the club would not open. This had the disadvantage that you could hear the music outside the club.

Usually at about 10 o'clock the phone behind the bar would ring, it would always be Mrs Muntus asking for me. "Hello Mrs Muntus how can I help you" I would always ask her, "we were wondering if you could kindly turn the music down a little since we can hear it quite clearly over here" she'd always request it, in a soft tone. Of course I can Mrs Muntus, while at the same time I'd be signalling to the DJ to turn it down, " how's' that" Mrs Muntus I always asked her " oh it's a lot better John and thank you very much". As she put the phone down I would dash over to the DJ and threaten him to keep it quiet for the next half an hour". One of the most popular drinks Carl served besides sparkling Champagne, which was given out on18th birthday parties was Pernod and Orange, he recalls " I still can't stand the smell of it after all these years, I must have sold gallons of it every week".

As part of the Charade's music policy they were still having live groups on at the club into the late 70's Carl clearly remembers seeing local Punk Rock groups there, but can't remember the names, although he still sees one of the drummers who now plays in a local Jazz band. Another well known local group that he remembers are My Pierrot Dolls a post punk new wave band who appeared there. As part of his training to become a chef he worked for one week on the food bar, "everything was deep fried as I remember, not much training but a lot of sweat stuck in that little kitchen for a week".

Punk Rock came upon the music industry not like a wave from across the Atlantic but more like a tsunami erupting in the record vaults. Suddenly record executives could be seen flying around the country looking to sign any band that resembled a Punk Rock group, and if you don't find any, stick a label on the ones you have that says "Punk Rock". Within a couple of years the punk rock phenomenon had subsided, with the last venue for new wave groups to appear live in the town "The Windmill Club" changing its musical policy away from such groups at the end of December 1977.

Bob Marley Tour. 1977

Rick Hardy was a close friend of Dinky Dawson, in 1967 he clearly remembers going over to the Wheel in Manchester with him to see a live band but as the years have passed he cannot remember the band's name, like Dinky he would work in the music industry but as a coach driver. "I worked for a coach company called Carnell's who at the time had the most luxurious coaches in the country and that is why all the big acts picked us for their European Tours. In 1977 I landed a dream job as the coach driver for Bob Marley's Exodus tour recalls Rick, little did I know at the time that I'd be the only white guy on the tour. My next big surprise was when Cindy Breakspeare turned up one day with some of the contestants from the Miss World competition, which she had won the previous year.

When Bob went on stage, I was usually given the job of looking after all the gear that was kept under the coach. This was usually, LPs, tee-shirts, tour magazines and whatever those Rastafarians' carried around with them. You'd usually get some guy trying to buy tee-shirts on the cheap off you, but I was having none of it. It was while I was on this tour that I got a phone call from home telling me that I was a dad for the first time. When I told the band they took me out to celebrate, that's me, the Rastafarians, Bob and the Wailers and all the Miss World contestants, it's the best night out I ever had and being the only white guy had its rewards that night. When I drove for The Byrds it was the first time that I came across the five star treatment. Everything was five star, food, hotels the way the promoters treated you, they even let my wife come and stay with me in London in our five star hotel.

During a gig with the Byrds in Manchester, Rick remembers seeing some lads from Rotherham, one of whom was Dave Halliday (Doc) in the crowd and introduced them all to the Band. Doc was responsible for opening the first Folk Club in the town called "Wheatsheaf Folk Club", which opened on Friday 25th February 1965 with Derroll Adams from America being the first act as Doc explains, "to us Derroll looked like an old man, he was 40 at the time and came up from London for the gig.

On the night he just sat and played his Banjo and sang without a mic and when two of my friends started talking I had no option but to throw them out, they were George Milnes (Jud) and Peter Didlock (Ped) they kept telling me they were members, but out they still went. Derroll stayed at my house that night and next day we all caught the bus to the railway station with him, when he got on the bus everyone was asking for his autograph.

It was the first time Rotherham had seen an American musician up close, with him wearing a Stetson hat and cowboy boots and carrying a Banjo case he really stood out". Derroll was a close friend of James Dean the movie star and also Dylan, appearing in the documentary film from 1967 about Dylan called 'Don't Look Back'.

Driving for Joe Cocker was different, he'd recently become a big star and with that came all the media attention, often we'd just sit down and talk about the clubs in Sheffield and Rotherham that he'd worked in, he even remembered the old Pendulum club from the sixties.

One of the best jobs I got was driving for Demis Roussos, he'd also just broken into the big time and it was this tour that he left his wife for a Miss World finalist, somehow bands just attracted'em. I used to call him Denis instead of Demis and after a couple of days his woman says to me "Rick he is Greek and his name is Demis, not Denis" I said I know he's Greek and I know his name and when he walked onto the coach I said, I've hung your Caftan at the back of the coach for you Denis. The rest of the tour I called him Denis, but he didn't seem to mind, she did though. It was at the end of the seventies that I found myself in Morocco and heard that Eric Dewsnap with Dave Manns, (his dad was big on the council in those days,) had bought into a camp site on the coast in Morocco near the border with Niger. I can still picture them both to this day when I turned up, they where both painting the side of huts on the site ready for the big influx of French tourists, that never arrived. As I explained, it may be a great beach to surf on and be secluded but its 200 miles from the airport". Eric would eventually move to London at the end of the Seventies, he explains why. "There was no work up here again, it was always boom or recession and it was recession again, so I packed up my gear and went to London. The first day there I was offered four jobs, I eventually ended up as a partner in a company that supplies and maintains all the software for recording equipment in Coroners Courts and The Magistrate Courts throughout the country". This year at the Arts centre on 28th January, we have the blonde soul singer Cissy Stone who performs live on stage in a lunch time Concert and the following Friday the entertainment is pre-war Berlin style, from a group called Cabaret Lunaire, "Music, satire, art and sophistication" is what they promise. Later in the same year we see another local DJ Steve Lindley join Gary Glitter for a two month tour of the UK. Steve had been working on and off for Gary since they first met in 1974 when Steve was working in Spain as a DJ.

John Kennedy DJ

John Kennedy was the Progressive Rock DJ on Wednesday nights during the punk rock scene. He first started out as a DJ with Sean Hampsey when he was fifteen, running a mobile disco in and around Thurcroft.

Sean and John were the Charades first double act as DJs; this meant that Sean could play Motown and Soul music during his spot while John concentrated on pop and rock music. Like most of the other DJs before them they both had day jobs, John was an apprentice tool maker at Stanley Tools.

After day release at college, which coincided with his Progressive Rock Nights he could be seen catching the bus from the town centre up to the Charade with a large box of records under his arm. Fortunately for him he would be able to share a taxi home with the other staff back to Thurcroft. "When I started at the Charade John Rose explained to me that my job at the club was to sell sex", "I told him straight I'm a DJ not a pimp".

This is where the Charade's music policy was explained to him. "The job of all our DJs is to keep the dance floor full and we leave it up to you what type of music to play, explained John, but at 11.45pm you put on slow records, so that the lads ask the birds they have been eyeing up all night to dance. If they both go home happy they'll come back again, that's how we sell sex". To John Kennedy this was all well and good, until you had a dance floor full of Maltby Rockers.

For over two years John and Sean had learned their trade as DJs in and around the mining communities by giving the public what they had paid for at private functions. John explained when working in and around Maltby. "The lads would stand at the bar all night and then dance the last half hour, after the alcohol had lubricated their brains like a thick coal tar".

One of the Charades unwritten policies was not to rent the club out to young people from Maltby for private functions. They had learnt from experience that it took too much policing from the door staff. John Kennedy describes one Thursday night when he was the DJ at a private function. "I'd been playing a mixture of music to keep the dance floor full and during the night I had a few altercations with some of the crowd who wanted more rock style music playing. At about 11.30pm the dance floor was getting full and with only thirty minutes to go I slowed the tempo down, it kicks off big style, the crowd are from Maltby".

This is no ordinary fight between groups of lads, they have only one enemy which is the club, they start to wreck it and the door staff soon realise this. John recounts that night. "Suddenly I see the bar staff and the bouncers come flying past me and into the office at the back of the DJ console with me as the last one in. As I'm shutting the door I suddenly remember my records so out I fly again and grab them.

For the next five minutes all we could hear was the sound of the club being trashed, then it all went quiet and as we peeked out from behind the door it looked like a scene from the western front. The club is empty; everything is destroyed with smoke rising up from the ashtrays on the floor". The night reminded John of the film called "Assault on Precinct 13" which came out the same year.

It was during one of the many private parties the Art College held at the Charade that over half of the students came dressed as Punk Rockers. This was the first time the club had come across this new rebellious, anti establishment music scene and within a few weeks Johns Popular Progressive rock nights on Wednesday had started to play Punk Rock. John explained. "Over a few months I'd built up a very popular Progressive Rock scene, seeing the club full to capacity by people who had come from as far as Leeds to a club that played real rock music, the word had got around Yorkshire that here was a club prepared to play their type of music.

Enter the punk rockers, I was told to start playing Punk Rock music on Wednesday nights and within a few weeks word had got around the grapevine that here was a club prepared to play Punk Rock. To the management both types of music sounded very similar, but to me and each tribal group it was as different as black and white. So all night both groups would be arguing amongst themselves and complaining to me that I'd already played too much of the others music, these became very heated nights which kept the doormen busy, especially when the punks started to spit at each other on the dance floor when Pogoing". Doorman Kevin Jackson hated to see this, but soon discovered that when threatened with eviction they soon stopped.

Kevin would work most private function nights. "John would always ask us at the weekend, what nights we would work for him? One weekend he asked me what I thought of Transvestites "that's a strange question to be asking a friend John". "It's only that a group of Transvestites' from Sheffield have booked the club next Thursday for a private party", said John. In the mid 1970's this was a very closed and secretive society because of the political and moral climate of the time, so no wonder they picked a club away from Sheffield. The DJ for the night was Bob Aiden who had started working at the club as a doorman, before becoming one of their DJs. Adie was the type of DJ that could get a dance floor full, no matter what type of crowd he had in and this night was no exception, they all went home with a smile on their faces, as did the staff.

Ady Dundas (SEE PHOTO)

Ady Dundas with Charade friends on the way home from an all-nighter in Wigan

The person in the foreground wearing the sheepskin is Ady Dundas from Selby, like Linda Kaye previously he would meet friends at the Charade before heading over to Wigan or Cleethorpes for the All-Nighters, but there the similarity ends. This photo was taken in 1977 at the services on the M62 coming back into Yorkshire from an all-night dance at Wigan. Ady had just been released from Armley Jail in Leeds after serving 29 months of a four year sentence for supplying drugs to the all-night soul scene. This is his story. "I left school at fifteen in 1967 and got a job in Selby at a paper mill, as an apprentice mechanical engineer. The firm I worked for had all types of tradesmen repairing everything in the factory including the building itself. About the same time one of my older sisters, I had two older and two younger sisters, was going out with a guy from Ramsgate. He was up here building the new power station. One summer he asked my parents if I could go back with him and my sister to Ramsgate for a week's holiday in the summer, being only fifteen I jumped at it. After we arrived at his parents he took me into Margate where all the action was, it blew me away, it was 1967 and was the first time I'd seen so many Mods all dressed in smart Italian suits with girlfriends all wearing short miniskirts and riding around on scooters. The next day I was in the barbers shop, having my long hair cut into the same style as the Mods, then round to a clothes shop to buy my first Ben Sherman shirt. I had become a mod over night. The rest of the holiday I spent hanging around in the cafes with them, listening to all the latest soul music on the juke boxes. As soon as I got back home I started to hang around 'Lynsey's Cafe' in Selby. Downstairs was the record shop and upstairs was the cafe. With all the older mods I used to go to The 'Boulevard Club' which was just outside Tadcaster on the A64. It was there that I saw Jimmy James and the Vagabonds, Geno Washington and J.J. Jackson. Sometimes I'd get a lift down to the Mojo in Sheffield; even then there was a sub culture amongst the mods of taking pills to keep awake when we went anywhere. Some weekends we would go over to the Wheel in Manchester, usually in someone's car, but as the older lads started to settle down and get married I started to hang around with those of my own age".

In 1971 the Twisted Wheel in Manchester closed down, Ady was only nineteen at the time, and like a lot of other soul fans started to look around for another all-nighter to fill his weekends. "Everybody knew everyone in Selby as Ady recounts, the all-nighters were becoming that popular in and around Selby that I started to run 40 or 50 seater coaches every weekend to either 'Up-the Junction' at Crewe or 'The Torch' in Stoke on Trent and the money I made would always pay for my night out. Because I was organising the coaches it was only natural for my friends to ask me to get them some gear for the night (pills), which I started to do and within a few weeks I was supplying nearly everyone on the coach.

It was down at the Torch that I got to know a lot of lads from Rotherham and within a few weeks I would be bumping into them in Selby at weekends with their new girlfriends. By the time The 'Va-Va' all-nighter opened in Bolton on Friday nights in 1973 a couple of us were supplying more than the Selby crowd with pills, in fact we used to carry all the pills around in a small black leather briefcase with bags full of pills for our customers.

On a normal weekend we'd sell about 1000 to 1200 pills. At the end of 1973 our supplier in Stockport got raided and the police found his diary with over twenty names, all his main customers and what their weekly order was, we were all busted. Looking back on it, when Wigan opened and the media made it front page headlines the authorities had to clamp down on us.

They could tolerate a few thousand every weekend taking pills but not Tens of thousands, so they had to make an example of us, which they did. When I appeared in The Magistrates Court in Selby, there were 29 of us. Most of them getting fined for possession, but five of us were sent to the Crown Courts at Doncaster for trial.

At the end of the trial I got four years as did three of my mates, but one got five years because he'd been stealing cars every weekend to get home. It was

Eric from Selby with friends

actually mentioned in court that the local plod from Selby couldn't work out why stolen cars from all over the north of England were getting abandoned every weekend in Selby? I next asked "did you make a lot of money out of this?", "no not really", he replied, we made enough so that we got all our gear free and being the local suppliers becomes a drug in itself.

When I got sent down I hated it for about six weeks and then I got used to the routine. I was working in the kitchens, so I saw loads of my mates from the nighter scene come through Armley that first year.

What had happened to us in and around Selby was happening all over the North of England. "Well it got you away from drugs for a few years" I mentioned, "no not really, I started to take Tabs of Acid that I was having smuggled in. They were inside my mince pies and you can buy and sell anything in jail if you've got the money".

After serving 29 months of his sentence he was released three months early on parole on the understanding that he did not associate with any of his former pals, Ady now describes those first few weeks of freedom. "After I'd been out a couple of weeks I was driving back from an all-nighter at Saint Ives near Peterborough when I saw a police car flashing his lights at me to pull over. I'd been swerving on the road because those in the back couldn't make up their minds which cafe to pull into one Sunday morning. I said that's done it, the police want me to stop, whereupon my mate John opened the glove compartment and inside is a bag full of gear. I just looked at him as my heart skipped a beat; I'll get sent back down if they find that I said. He managed to shove it under his jacket as the police officer arrived. "you look lost sir" he said, "I am a bit, I replied, we're on our way home from a private party in Peterborough", where upon he said, "you all look done in sir, if I was you I'd pull into that cafe over there and get a few hours kip". "That was the luckiest escape I ever had".

Back home Ady finds it difficult to get a job. "We all found it hard at first, then someone gave me a new start at a local engineering firm in Selby. After leaving there I set up a local plumbing/ heating engineering company with a work mate before moving into buying and selling Antiques' this was about twenty years ago. A few years ago though, I could see it wasn't going to be as profitable, so I moved into property". "So you're still wheeling and dealing" I said as we sat in his Georgian Manor house with its walled garden", "yep" he replied.

The Policeman's Ball

A popular and local policeman who often called in at the club when he was on duty was Pc Kettlebrough. He was described by all who knew him as "a policeman who had gone in to policing to look after his community as a beat bobby". When on duty he would call into the club for his nightcap, he would stand at the top of the stairs, with his helmet off drinking his coffee. As John recounts "occasionally we'd ring him up if there was any trouble outside, he'd always part them and say, "you go home that way and you in the opposite direction". If one of them said but I don't live that way, "if you don't walk that way, how do you fancy spending a night in the cells", he would always reply and off they would go, walking the long way home.

Mark Kay another doorman from 1979, his twin brother worked behind the bar, remembers one Thursday night when they were having the annual policeman's ball. "From my vantage point at the top of the stairs, I noticed a patrol car pull up across from the club with its lights out. It was still there half an hour later so I had a word with Pc Kettlebrough. He went over with another officer and two minutes later the car sped off with lights blazing. When they got back I asked them, is it all sorted, "Put it this way, no one will be breathalysed within a two mile radius of this club tonight", came back the reply".

One cockney punter who had just arrived in town, via Australia found it very different, when after one night in the club he was stopped for driving around the roundabout without his lights on, John Habbin ended up being breathalysed and found to be well over the limit, his long-time friend Pete Kelly from Thurcroft would always play safe and get the bus home.

By 1978 John's loyal following of Progressive music lovers had convinced John Rose to have Friday nights as their night, with Saturday nights for disco/ funk/ soul music.

In September 'The Royal Shakespeare Company' tour the provinces and come to South Yorkshire for the first time ever. The company was formed in 1961 and after seventeen years of subsidies from the people of the region they perform twice in Sheffield and once at the Civic Theatre with an anthology of English poetry and prose called "Is there Honey still for tea?" It is the brain-child of actor Ian McKellan, from Burnley.

In the same week Jazz lovers of all ages witnessed a great sell out concert by George Melly at Clifton Hall; it was sponsored by Radio Sheffield and the local council. George Melly's final concert in June 2007 was at 'The 100 Club' in London, which by the way is as small inside as the Charade was.

Over at the Arts centre in the same week Opera lovers had a special treat when Derek Blackwell, the well-known Tenor from 'The Royal Opera House' Covent Garden appeared live, Derek was brought up in Staincross near Barnsley.

At the end of 1978 The "Sound of Music" record shop is voted the best record shop in South Yorkshire, this is the same shop that for the last 10 years had been supplying the Charade's DJs with their records. The owners Cyril and Muriel Charles won a long weekend in Nice

Disco Demolition Night, American style?

As one generation moves out, another generation moves into the Charade with its own style of music and dress.

By 1979 Disco music is still all the range on Saturday nights at the Charade. On Friday nights we have Rick Stuart playing the latest in Jazz/ Funk and on Mondays it's John Malkin, with Kaptain Kremmen on Wednesday nights. By March of 1979 the 'June Tyrell' school of dancing had three evenings dedicated to young dancers who wanted to learn to dance the John Travolta way. Radio stations across America were dedicated to playing disco/ Bee Gee's records 24 hours a day and what goes up must come down?. Welcome to "Disco Demolition Night", American style. By 1979 the Disco industry in America accounted for up to 40% of records in the singles charts, it dictated fashion, hairstyles and lifestyles, and it was worth an estimated four billion dollars.

Steve Dahl a popular Chicago DJ was fired from his radio station for refusing to play Disco orientated records in place of his rock albums.

Subsequently he was hired by a rival radio station, from where he carried on his campaign against Disco music. When asked by Mike Veeck to devise a promotional gimmick to promote a baseball game between the Detroit Tigers and Chicago White Sox for July 12th he hit on the idea of allowing people to bring unwanted disco records to the game in exchange for a 98 cent admission fee. On the night in question they would normally have a crowd of 12,000, in a stadium built for 52,000, but 90,000 turned up.

During a lull in the game which was broadcast live he had a large crate full of records rigged with explosives and placed in the middle of the stadium. Dahl entered the field dressed in army fatigues and helmet; he then led the crowd with chants of "disco sucks", before starting the countdown. The explosion tore a hole in the pitch showering spectators with vinyl and starting a riot, it was also responsible for starting similar anti-disco events across the country. Nile Rodgers guitarist and producer for the disco group Chic explained "It felt to us like Nazi book-burning. This is America, the home of rock and jazz and now people are afraid even to say the word disco".

Within weeks, night clubs had stopped playing disco music; record labels fired producers, song writers, singers and groups, they distanced themselves from disco music altogether. But in a warehouse, in a rundown part of Chicago through the burning embers of disco, another form of dance music was born, welcome to House Music courtesy of DJ Frankie Knuckles.

On the 21st September 1979 the Charade held its 11th Anniversary party, with DJs Rick Stuart and John Malkin. They also advertise for the first time ever in the Rotherham "The Happy Hour"with drinks at 27p.

With music evolving all the time and dance music in the UK no different; it starts to take a new path, New Romanticism is born. It rejects the austerity and anti fashion stance of punk with its fashion based on romantic themes in the style of the English Romantic period. (a breed of painters from 1847). Annie Lennox in an interview on Woman's Hour encapsulated the legacy of Punk Rock music on the music scene in the mid to late 70's when she said "It was like a hurricane blowing through the music industry, it blew away all the old pop groups and allowed a new generation of young talent to come through". In America the first Hip Hop record is released called Rappers Delight by The Sugarhill Gang, it is reputed to have sold five million records worldwide.

In October of this year Heavy Rock returns to the Charade on Monday nights, back by popular demand as Mark Kaye remembers" Monday nights were hectic with the club packed to the ceiling with Students in for free and half price

THE RALPH PITMAN PAGE

Battle of Bean... 1985

Late night bars ruling
NIGHTCLUB DRINKS PRICES WARNING

Drinks prices in local night clubs are likely to go up soon — and the owners are pretty annoyed about it.

This follows a recent House of Lords interpretation of the 1964 Licensing Act.

It says, in effect, that the public cannot fetch their own drinks from bars after the normal licensing time — which is 10.30 p.m. in the Rotherham area.

The farcical result is that night clubs throughout the country are having to set on waitresses to ferry drinks to customers after that time.

Local police are not pushing owners, but it is expected that all clubs in this area will be operating the "no drinks at the bar after 10.30" rule within a few weeks.

The new ruling has angered night club operators, who have collected a fighting fund to finance moves to get the law changed.

One such operator is Dave Allen, Managing Director of A and S Dance Promotions Ltd., who own 10 nightspots, including the Charade and the Adam and Eve in Rotherham.

"It is crazy," he said, "If a person is entitled to have a drink after 10.30, does it matter how he is served with it?"

And he warned that the extra expense of employing waitresses would have to be passed on to customers.

"I think that most clubs will charge 1p extra per drink after 10.30 to compensate," he said.

VS & Plays Concerts Films

SPECTRUM

Rita Atkinson

MEMBERSHIP No. **15**

No. **979**

Tiffany's
Main Street, Rotherham

Monday Super Scene Monthly Pass

will admit the holder to TIFFANY'S any Monday during MAY at the reduced price of 15p before 10 p.m. Over 18s only

Signature *Rita Atkinson*

This pass is no guarantee of admission as the Management reserve the right to refuse admission without any given reason. This pass can be withdrawn at any time.

Scot. Auto. Edin

drinks all night long" he describes one night in particular " I was standing on the step near the fire exit which gave me a good view of the club when this couple suddenly disappeared, so I walked over to where I had last seen them and noticed this large pile of overcoats in the corner moving up and down to the rhythm of the music. I tapped the coats and told them to pack it in and both times they told me to F off, by this time another doorman had arrived, "so we pulled the coats off and tried to frog march him out, whereupon he fell onto a table as soon as we let go of him. He started to complain saying we'd pushed him until he noticed his trousers around his ankles, after we'd got rid of him his girl friend started to complain so out she went too".

Next week John got a letter as Mark remembers "her dad, who was some local big wig is complaining how his daughter was manhandled out of the club and is coming down to see John, so John nipped it in the bud with a phone call describing the night as tactically as he could".

In November we have a rare visit to the Arts Centre by the best-selling author Douglas Adams, whose book "Hitch- Hiker's Guide to the Galaxy" is topping the book charts, it would go on to sell 14 million copies worldwide.

Rick Stuart DJ, Record Producer and Radio One Producer

Rick Stuart, whose parents knew Brian Blessed and Tony Christie went to Oakwood School. He started his career at the age of sixteen when he became the clubs youngest ever DJ. As he explained, "since the age of twelve I'd been collecting vinyl records and at fifteen I'd already been to the all-night dancers at Wigan Casino.

One night in the Charade John Rose asked me if I'd like a go because the DJ was late or couldn't make it. It went down so well that they offered me a job, eventually moving me to the Friday night spot. At first I lied about my age and I must have looked old enough since at the time I had a moustache. I can remember Dave Growns going crazy with me when over a year later I held my 18th birthday bash there".

Like all teenagers from the Charade, some weekends they would hire a coach for the night and shoot over to Manchester to a night club called "Pips", as Rick remembers. "The club was great and what we all liked about it compared to the Charade is that it had four separate dance floors on different levels, catering to all types of music at the time, so you could have an hour of Roxy music then down a level for Jazz/Funk, then into another room for New wave etc".

This was the year that the film Quadrophenia was released which spurred a big revival in the Mod culture as Rick recalls. "Because the music at the time was changing so fast, we'd have different tribes in wanting to listen and dance to only their music, which at the time created a lot of friction in the club.

Being a DJ taught you how to calm groups of drunken lads down and when that failed I'd turn to the fire extinguishers which always made them back off". As Rick remembered "it was a great time in all our lives being students at 'Thomas Rotherham College', studying for our 'A' levels in the day and spending the nights at the Charade, though our parents thought differently, but looking back on it 30 years later it all worked out for us all. As a Saturday job I was working in the market at the Sound of Music record stall, but after a few months I set up my own store, as I remember it was my first venture as an entrepreneur.

On Friday nights I'd play a mixture of Jazz/Funk music from groups like Earth Wind and Fire, Funkadelic, Kool and the Gang and Parliament. To anyone coming to the club for the first time it was like a Tardis in reverse, it looked big on the outside but small on the inside.

At the weekends we knew how to pack them in, with usually over 300 teenagers in there'd be no room on the dance floor and I would often see someone holding a drink while talking to friends and five minutes later they'd moved apart due to the ebb and flow of the crowd. To me as a DJ the club was always on the edge, it was on the edge of town, the music was always on the edge and some nights the punters would go over the edge!"

Rick remembers trying to mix the records with the decks. "Rap music had just come onto the scene and I'd try mixing the records with the old twin decks, this meant slowing one record down by pressing down on the record deck to make it go slower while playing the other at its normal speed, if it worked it sounded great, but when it didn't everyone would stop dancing and look at you".

When he left the Charade in 1980 it was to go to University at Kingston Poly in Kingston upon Thames, London. Rick then went on to do a Post Graduate course at The National Broadcasting School in Soho London for 18 months. This college had been set up to provide the creative production executives and on air talent for local radio which was in the process of being deregulated. Once back in the real world he decided to go freelance as he remembers "this gave me the option of working for several local radio stations while at the same time producing for bands, since the days had gone when a drummer and a few guitars were all that a band needed, nowadays with the synthesisers they needed a lot more High Tech support to produce an album".

By 1986 Rick had got a job at Radio One. "All the training and studying had come together and I had landed myself a job as a freelance 'Radio One Executive Producer' working with Bruno Brookes until 1989". He also found himself working alongside Mark Goodier and Paul Gambaccini and Kid

Jenson while at the BBC. Because he was working freelance, it gave him the opportunity to work with the Music Factory on their 1989 LP "Jive Bunny", where he was heavily involved with the production and mixing work. This LP had three consecutive number one hits, but as he soon learned "where there's a hit there's a writ as they say in the music industry".

After his degree he also found time to work as a DJ at the Adam and Eve before finally moving down to Ipswich which he used as a base to commute into London, since it was only 70 miles by train into the capital. "Before I left to go 'A and S' called me in one day to ask why I was leaving? After I'd explained that I wanted a career in the Media and was moving to Ipswich they said "we're thinking of opening a Casino in Ipswich, we'll give you a ring in a couple of weeks and you can tell us what the night life is like". This I did, I told them it's like being in the 1950's, so 'A and S' never did move down there.

He remembers one of the perks as a DJ in the Charade was that "the record companies in London would send me promotional records on white labels to try out in the club and I'd report back how they went down".

It became known in the record industry as "Record Pluggers" they would use the dance clubs to build up a following for an artist before releasing the record, thereby guaranteeing it to go straight into the charts.

At the age of 28 Rick now took a different path in his life, "rather than just be involved in producing records and working with bands on tracks, I decided it was time to make some money for myself and with my background I set up a company providing in flight entertainment for companies like Air Tours, Britannia and British Airways.

This I expanded to provide aviation hardware and communication expertise to the airline industry". In 2012 his company with the Scottish company Avilt launched the first ever wireless screen for airline passengers offering multi functional entertainment options, (in plain English the screen on the back of an airline seat is hardwired, whereas theirs is not, it will also give the passenger more entertainment options). It also saves a lot of weight on a wide bodied jet, up to 1.5 tons and is a lot easier to maintain. Not bad for a Charade DJ.

We end the 70's decade with the news that in China, they are to restrict families to one child per couple; this resulted in an estimated 400 million less children over the next 30 years being born in China.

Chapter 3
A new Decade, the '80s.

Nigel Blease DJ

Nigel started going to the Charade while still only seventeen, he first remembers going to the Rock Nights with others from the Art college, as Nigel explained, "We always used the Charade for birthday parties and Christmas dances as well, mainly because of the clubs relaxed door policy, which meant that for young students between sixteen and eighteen years of age you got into the club. At one Christmas dance we all arranged to meet in the Stag pub across the road at 7 o'clock, but as we drifted in the landlord 'John Wayne' had other ideas. He told us that "he wasn't having his pub full of layabout students" and threw us all out, even though a lot were mature students".

At the age of seventeen Nigel and Andrew Watt from college had started a mobile disco, out of the back of a Reliant Robin three wheeler. Nigel explains "because we had a friend at the Steely Quarry in Derbyshire most weekends we would be driving around the Peak District with the back of the Reliant loaded down with decks, amplifiers and boxes full of records, how the front wheel stayed on the road when going up those steep hills still amazes me to this day. After six months of the Pennines I decided to try and get a job at the Charade because I lived only a mile away. After wearing John Rose down I got a break when one of the regular DJs was away on holiday".

Always on the lookout for new up and coming talent John was quick to give him a night at the weekend. Like most of the DJs at the Charade, Nigel played music that was ahead of its time, whereas in the town the other clubs played music mainly from the charts.

The DJs at the Charade would be forever searching for the latest up and coming bands of the day. "Groups like Duran Duran, the B52s, Japan and the Lambrettas, we'd be playing weeks before they broke into the main stream, recalls Nigel, to us the Charade was a sign post for new music not a dead end like the other clubs in town". The Lambrettas appeared at the Clifton Hall on Thursday 15th of May 1980, with The Circles as support, they even had an early show for under 18's. This was an era when a new type of music was breaking, which happened in Sheffield one night at the Top Rank. Nigel goes on to explain. "We all went up to Sheffield one night to see the Stranglers and the supports act The

Skids, who had to pull out. After a frantic search around the city for a support act, a little known group called The Human League were booked". Nigel now tells us about one of those defining times in musical history. "When the 'Human League' came on with those synthesisers it just blew you away, where as they had only been used a little on some records, here was a group using them all the time, we all knew then that this was the future".

During this period those from RCAT College in the town centre, who were mostly former Oakwood school pupils could be seen at the Charade and occasionally they would travel down to the Rum Runner in Birmingham. One night Nigel and his Art School crowd managed to see live at the Rum Runner Pete Shelley, one of the founding members of The Buzzcocks.

Other groups that launched their careers form this club besides Duran Duran were Dexy's Midnight Runners, UB40 and The Beat. Sadly the club was demolished in 1987 to make way for the Hyatt Hotel.

Closer to home the Charade crowd could be seen regularly at the Limit in Sheffield, as Nigel remembers. "It was a great time for new bands, especially at the Limit in Sheffield, a crowd of us from the club would regularly see unheard of bands there, within a few weeks I'd be playing their first single on Friday nights courtesy of the Sound of Music and one month later it would be in the charts".

One of the most popular records that Nigel remembers playing in 1981 was "Kick in the Eye" by the gothic rock band "Bauhaus", as he says "it could be guaranteed to fill the dance floor". At the end of 1980 the musical word is thrown into disbelief when John Lennon was shot dead on the 8th December in New York.

Paul Shane (who lived next door to Des Pejko in Shaftsbury Square in the 50's) a well known local comedian and former miner is catapulted to stardom when he stars in the hit TV series Hi-Di-Hi as Ted Bovis, the camp compere. It is broadcast on 26 February 1981 and runs for 58 episodes, finally finishing on the 30 June 1988; the first pilot show was broadcast on 1st January 1980.

By the middle of 1981 we have Heavy Rock Nights on Mondays with Captain Kremmen, Friday nights is Nigel Blease and on Saturday nights we have Disco music with John Malkin and Dave D. Dexter. Nigel explained "I was earning as much money being a DJ for two nights as I was for 40 hours at work, so I gave up the day job".

In October of 1981 the Charade got a new owner when Dave Allen sold the club to Keith Wilson, a car salesman. By now Dave Allen was on his way to becoming a multi millionaire and with great reluctance he lets go of the club where it all started, twelve years previously. The gamble that he took in 1968 had paid off, but all the memories of thousands of teenagers would live on forever.

The new owner Keith Wilson decides to keep the name of the club and the same logo as used in the Advertiser for the time being. Steve Lindley becomes the resident DJ on Saturday nights; he first started his career at the LBJ club before moving onto the Boardwalk which was situated at the YMCA building. Carl Eggleston recounts, "Steve was great at getting the dance floor full with everyone buzzing and around 10 o'clock he'd move down to the Adam and Eve, to do the same there". Steve Lindley was the first DJ to leave the area when in May of 1971 he went to work in Majorca as a DJ with his Go Go dancer girlfriend Denise Christmas.

In September 1977 he was working for Gary Glitter whom he first worked for in Spain in 1974. This time as Steve explained to the Advertiser "I'll be his personal assistant spending most of my time chauffeuring Gary around in his Rolls Royce, there's a lot more to do when I'm with the band because there are five of them and they are more demanding, but with Gary there are just the two of us and we're good mates. He's a really nice bloke and we always stay in the top hotels and invariably throw a party after each show".

Also this year we have the death of Bill Haley who died on the 9th February 1981, he is credited by many as popularizing Rock and Roll in its infancy with his world wide hit record "Rock Around the Clock", which was first released in 1954 but became a worldwide hit when it was the sound track for a film called "Blackboard Jungle" which came out in 1955. Another one of his great hits "Shake Rattle and Roll" was the first ever Rock and Roll song to enter the British charts in December of 1954.

One of the biggest selling records of 1981 was "Tainted Love" by Soft Cell; it would go on to be number one in seventeen countries worldwide. It was first released in 1964 by Gloria Jones; yes the same Gloria Jones of Marc Bolan fame. It first became popular on the Northern Soul scene in 1974 at the all-nighters in Wigan, but with the first report of Aids in Los Angeles on the 5th June 1981 the lyrics took on a different meaning. On the 17th of December we have Chris Bonington the famous mountaineer giving a talk on the 1st ascent in China of 'Mount Kongur' at Clifton Hall.

NEW LOOK

Charade

STAG ROUNDABOUT, ROTHERHAM 72942
We, the Management, have pleasure in
announcing our
**12th ANNIVERSARY
FANCY DRESS PARTY**
Saturday, November 15th

HATS, STREAMERS, PRIZES AND SURPRISES
Admission FREE with this advert
(Fancy Dress optional)
— plus anyone in Fancy Dress also FREE

NEW LOOK

Charade

154 WICKERSLEY ROAD, ROTHERHAM · TEL 72942
**JOIN US SATURDAY NIGHT
AND HEAR ROTHERHAM'S
NO 1 DJ IN ACTION**

THE INIMITABLE
"STEVE LINDLEY"

THE CHARADE IS ALSO AVAILABLE FOR
YOU PRIVATE HIRE
"AT LAST YEAR'S RATES"

P.s.: We require part time staff
for details ring John or Dave on Rotherham
72942
SEE YER SOON

THE RALPH PITMAN PAGE

On tour with the big G

Steve Lindley, the former Rotherham D.J., begins a big
two-months tour as personal assistant to the Big G — Gary Glitter
— this week-end.

Twenty-eight years old Steve, who will be remembered from the
old Pendulum and Oasis clubs, started working for the Glitter Band i
1974 after meeting Gary in Spain.

Since then he has
travelled all over the
world with the band, rising
from the more mundane
jobs like trouser pressing
to the more demanding
tasks of tour manager.

It was in February and
March that Gary Glitter
made his comeback tour
and Steve was offered the
job of accompanying him
as his personal aide.

After the tour, Gary
went back to his big
country house and Steve
rejoined the band for a
British tour, followed by
recording sessions.

Recently he was in
Rotherham for a holiday
but then it was back to
London where Gary began

three weeks of rehearsals
with session musicians for
his next tour.

That begins this week-
end and ends on
December 4th, starting
with a week at Batley
Variety Club.

Steve, who will spend
much of his time
chauffeuring the singer
in his Rolls Royce, says
he's looking forward to it.

"There is a lot more to
do when I'm with the band
because there are five of
them and they are more
demanding," he said.

"With Gary there are
just the two of us and
we're good mates. He's a
really nice bloke.

Gary always stays in

top hotels and invaria
throws a party after e
show.

"And he really is
champagne diet. He u
watches what he's e
before a tour to
down."

Steve says there
of an Australian t
Gary next year,
doesn't envisage stayi…
his current line of work
permanently.

"I don't want to be a
star or anything because
after two or three years
you've blown it." he said.

"What I'd really like to
break into is production
work or perhaps writing
— something behind the
scenes."

EVERY NIGHT in the PAVILION
DISCO from 10.30
ADMISSION £3

**TONIGHT, FRIDAY
RADIO ONE DJ**

Paul Gambaccini

108

The picture on the 'Front Cover' of this book was taken in Skegness on an Easter bank holiday in 1971; it is a group of teenagers from the Charade. By 1981 all the teenagers would be in their late 20's most of them would be married and bringing up families of their own. They had all gone to Skegness for the Bank Holiday, with most of them sleeping rough with only a sleeping bag to keep them warm at night.

Every Bank Holiday there would be a great exodus from the towns and cities to the coast by thousands of teenagers and there is always safety in numbers. Some of them would have brushes with the law as they grew older but all would eventually settle down.

Two of them would go on to great things; one is Keith Oxley who would be responsible for maintaining the machine that dug the channel tunnel and the other is Norman Bettison who would go on to join the Police Force in 1972. He would rise rapidly through the ranks and by January 2007 had become The Chief Constable of West Yorkshire. Steve Cavill, a close friend of Norman remembers them going to watch Rotherham play York City in York one night. On the way out of York the supporters' bus was stoned and all the windows were broken. He also remembered them doing the conga around the Stag Roundabout one New Years Eve as well. Along his journey through the police force he would obtain a Master's Degree in Philosophy and Psychology from Oxford University and a Master's Degree in Business Administration from Sheffield Hallam University. In 2006 he was awarded a Knighthood in the Queens Birthdays Honours list. He is now Sir Norman Bettison, but as we look at the photograph from 1971 we must never forget that we were all teenagers once.

Nigel Wainwright, Doorman

Nigel started work at the club in 1975. "At the time I was a mechanic mainly repairing lorries and decide to save up and buy my own garage. I worked at the club until 1982 and I remember Keith Wilson changing the layout of the club, with the four TV screens and new dance floor it gave the club an upmarket feel. I would work at my day job and then work on average five nights a week for seven years until I had the money to buy my own garage.

One Christmas Eve I refused entry to someone because he looked drunk, about an hour later he tried again and John Rose said. "We'll let him in since its Christmas and keep an eye on him" which we did. At the end of the night we found him sat on his own so naturally we walked him downstairs. We left him stood up outside the club as we jumped into a taxi down to the Eve. Next day while I was at home having my Christmas dinner, two plain clothes police officers came down our drive. They arrested me because they had found a dead person outside of the Charade and knew that I worked there. After four hours questioning I was released and had to appear at the Coroner's inquest a few weeks later. Apparently I'd been arrested because the body had been covered in bruises, which led the police to assume that I /we had beaten him up.

The Coroner explained to his family that he had died due to a mixture of alcohol and tablets, the side effect being that his body was covered in what looked like bruises. It's something I never want to live through again. On some nights especially in the summer I'd find up to 20 teenagers on the flat roof next to the fire exit waiting to try and get in free, what made it worse was that there was no handrail around the roof saving you from a 20 ft drop".

1982 starts with "My Pierrot Dolls" live at the Charade on Wednesday January 13th. This is the year that the name of the club changed to "Formula One Club" as Keith Wilson recounts. "I'd had the club for about a year and decided it needed a complete refit, so I had it redesigned as an American style Disco with the latest in high technology entertainment which included the first ever video screens in a night club in the area. I also decided to keep the three main DJs who were Steve Lindley, Dave Wadkin and John Malkin plus all the other staff. I picked the name for the club because I had been a semi professional racing driver in Single Seat formula Ford cars up until 1975, when I retired through injuries".

His oldest son Justin followed in his father's footsteps racing in Formula One in 2003 along side Mark Webber at Jaguar-Cosworth, he now races Indi cars in America. The early '80s was a period when music was changing every six to twelve months, there was still disco, funk, rock music, post punk, new wave etc etc and the 'Formula One' catered for every one with their state of the art video screens as Nigel Blease recalls. "There were four Sony TV's, one in each corner and when rewinding the VHF videos you could see them going backwards on the screens. If we didn't have a video to match the record we'd put on 'Bruce Lee' films that John Rose had supplied".

He also remembers the brand new decks. The club was the first in the area to have twin decks that you could slow down or speed up, so that one record could be synchronised as it finished with the one just starting". This new technology was made possible when the Beats per Minute, (BPM) was stamped on the records or published in the Musical Express. Nigel explained. "Sometimes you had to get a stop watch out and count the BPM as it was playing and then make a note on the record, which made mixing records a lot easier. On some nights Nigel could be seen in the club dressed all in black as he reminds us "I'd wear black trousers and jacket with a black shirt and tie, black shoes, black hat, drinking a black drink and smoking black Russian cigarettes, while the women wore Pencil black skirts and white blouses".

Also this year Carl moved down to London to find work as a chef, he recounts " In the early 80's there was no work up here, everything was closing down, so I moved to London to find work and shared a flat with Lisa Wowk whom I knew from the Charade". Lisa was described by everybody who met her, as one of the most attractive women of the 80's. Carl picks up his London story "Lisa had contacts all over the capital and got me my first job as a chef in a Top London Hotel.

When Christmas came around it was hectic with us working 18 hours a day in hot sweaty kitchens and the only way to keep awake was by taking the pills. They handed these around every day. We'd take three in the morning, followed by three in the afternoon and finally three at night, just to keep awake". The pills were Amphetamines, as Carl remembers, Lisa would go on to marry the England rugby captain Will Carling.

When Carl came back up north he would meet and marry Margaret Charles, whose parents ran the Sound of Music record shop.

In November of 1982 Keith Wilson has a new manager after John Rose decides to leave the night club scene and get a daytime job.

He is replaced by Peter Smith who becomes the manager as well as working full time as a miner, he said. "I didn't think that there was so much work to do running a small club, I'd arrive home from the pit about 2 o'clock, have some lunch and hot foot it to the Formula One Club, my first job being to carry all the barrels of beer and lager up two flights of stairs at the back of the building. The first couple weren't too bad but by the time you'd done four or five you were all in".

The three main DJs in 1982 were Pete Duke, John Malkin and Nigel Blease.

"I and Keith were into our early 30's, so we decided to leave the music policy to the DJs and I was to concentrate on looking after the staff with the general maintenance of the club thrown in.

At this time Keith was also running a car showroom so he didn't have too much spare time for the club" said Peter. One of the changes we made was when we introduced a "Kids Night" on Wednesday nights for fourteen to seventeen year olds.

On December 17th 1982 we have a rare visitor to the town when no other than Radio One DJ Paul Gambaccini is on at The Carlton Park Hotel for one night only.

A Good Night's Sleep

As happens with all clubs, as Pete Smith and John Rose recalled, "when the youngsters first started coming to the club we'd see them every weekend and even in the week and as they got older, we would see less of them, especially when it was someone's birthday they would use the clubs in Sheffield". Two such teenagers' where Tom Burton and Mart Scott. "For a change we all decided to go to Sheffield one Saturday night and rather than walk home we would catch the mail train from Sheffield to the town centre which only took fifteen minutes", explained Mart. "When we got to the station just after one in the morning there were hundreds waiting for the train and we were lucky to get a seat. I remember the journey home with the rhythmic motion of the train as it went click-ity-click over the rails, as I opened my eyes and saw the sun rising I nudged Tom and said they've left us asleep on the train, where are we?". He looked out of the window and replied "we're near Leeds; wake me when we pull into the station". Ten minutes later I was shaking him "we're pulling into Carlisle railway station; we're 200 miles from home".

They had no money so had to throw themselves on the mercy of the station master, Fat controller as Tom recounts. "We explained our predicament to him and asked "when's the next train back to Sheffield?", "tomorrow" he replied, but how do we get home today I want to know". "You'll have to catch a train to Newcastle and then down to Sheffield from there he replied, you won't get lost, just as long as you can see Hadrian's Wall from the train window". So a five mile railway journey had turned into a 500 mile round trip, taking over18 hours to get home

1983

The Formula One Club still have Monday nights as the Heavy Rock nights with ½ price drinks all night and on the 25th August the club starts a Rock and Roll night on Wednesday nights. This is the first time ever that music from the late 50's/ early 60's was ever played at the club in fifteen years.

One night as the club is about to open a local resident calls in to see the manager with a complaint. "Last night I could hear something in my garden moving about, when I looked out of the window there was a couple from this club making love on my lawn" he said. Keith the manager asked him "what on the back lawn", "no on the front lawn, what are you going to do about it" he asked. "There's nothing we can do" explained Keith.

One month later the same person was back again. "I've caught another couple

Keith's No 1 formula for nightclub success

An American-style disco offering the latest in high technology entertainment has opened in Rotherham.

The Formula One Club at the Stag roundabout has been fully equipped with the most modern sound and light system available, including three video screens.

Owner of Formula One, also owner of K. R. Wilson Garages Ltd, Mr Keith Wilson, is a former semi-professional racing driver.

He retired as a driver of single seater formula Ford cars through injuries in 1973.

Mr Wilson bought the club in October last year.

Other new features are the custom built ultra-violet lights, a system of mirrors and coloured lights fitted into the roofs.

Fibre-optic lights and holographic lights have been installed over the new, larger dance floor with a fog machine to complete the effect.

New furnishings and decorations complete the look of the Formula One Club, which was formerly the Charade.

"It's a very popular feature of the club, because it means we can offer something for everyone," said Mr Wilson.

The three resident disco jockeys have a newly fitted disco console and provide entertainment on Monday, Thursday, Friday and Saturday each week.

The DJs are Steve Lindley, Dave Wadkin and John Malkin.

The Formula One Club can be hired for private parties and discos on Tuesdays and Wednesdays.

...and gave it a new image to make it one of the most popular nightspots in town.

The club offers video entertainment and also passes use of cameras to cover live dancing.

Another... at the club each week... heavy rock music night on Mondays, when drinks are sold at half price from 8pm to 10pm.

You can also complete your evening with a basket meal from the club's Earl Bar. Meals on the menu include scampi and chips and chicken and chips—at a bargain at 99p each.

The Formula One Club is open from 8pm to midnight to over 18s and the management ask for reasonably smart dress.

The Formula One Club is the first nightclub Mr Wilson has owned, and a great deal of hard work has gone into creating its new image.

Mr Wilson added he would strive to maintain the number one formula.

FORMULA ONE CLUB
(FORMERLY CHARADE)
Stag Roundabout, Rotherham. Tel 72942

FOR THE
BEST IN AUDIO
& VIDEO ENTERTAINMENT

MON HEAVY ROCK NIGHT
See John Malkin, one of our resident DJs in action
½ PRICE DRINKS 8pm-10pm

TUES & WED Available for Private Functions,
Birthdays, Engagements, etc.

THURS Now open every Thursday by popular demand.
Resident DJ Dave Wadkin

FRI Get the weekend off to a flying start with the best
sounds and sights around.

SAT Be a winner!
Join Steve Lindley at the FORMULA ONE CLUB.
BY POPULAR DEMAND WE ARE OPEN EVERY THURSDAY 8pm Midnight

last night making love" he said, "not on the front lawn again" asked Keith, "no this time they broke into my car on the drive since it was raining, they were both naked on the back seat, what are you going to do about it ?" . Keith walked away as one of the bouncers said "I wish we had a camera".

Also this year My Pierrot Dolls who had appeared at the club when it was called the Charade have reformed with new members joining the last two original members Ivor Hillman and Barry Thurman. They are to start rehearsing with a view to making 1984 the 'Year of the Dolls'. Their big break came when they reached the finals of "Battle of the Bands" at Sheffield University alongside five other bands. The winners of this prestigious competition would go on to represent Yorkshire in the finals at London. They had organised support from Dale Farm Foods at Rawmarsh, a coach full of fellow workers had gone along to give vocal support. The night ended as do most outings from Rawmarsh with a fight, with the students from the university. They were subsequently banned from the competition.

By 1984 the Club had managed to get its drink licence extended to 1am as Keith explained. "The competition in the town was open till 2 am most nights and it was the only way that we found to keep the youngsters of the area from drifting into town, especially at the weekends".

It was still Heavy Rock nights on Mondays, with the weekend advertised as 'Disco Night' with the DJ still John Malkin and Tom Morrell.

The club was still getting packed to the ceiling, the main attraction being the Video Entertainment system that Keith had installed two years previously, as he explained. "Some nights at the weekend the club seemed to come alive as the night wore on, with the dance floor full of dancers moving to the rhythm and beat of the music, condensation would seep into the ceiling and walls of the club, awakening past memories, spanning sixteen years of music with the beating heart of the club still the dance floor. As the DJ built the atmosphere up the energy and sweat of the dancers would add another layer to the club, like a teenager grows another layer of skin. To every generation of teenagers that went this was the pinnacle of the clubs reputation.

Jill Graver from Wickersley

As a teenager, we always used to go there. In fact, it was the first night club I ever went to, I think I was fourteen! We always used to have parties there when we were in the 6th form and could walk back to Wickersley. If we went to Tiffany's in town we would have to get a taxi or sweet talk somebody's dad into picking us up. God knows how we got in when we were so young. We thought we looked grown up but I doubt we did. I remember the boys used to get turned away. They didn't have the advantage of make up to make them look older. We used to catch the bus dressed up to the nines, pay a 2p child fare and then head off to the Formula One! I did get together there with my future husband and father of my children one night just before my 18th birthday in 1985. I can even remember that we danced to 'Easy Lover'.... not the most romantic of songs. I can remember what he was wearing; it was one of those thin leather ties that were all the rage. Unfortunately we are no longer married but if it weren't for the Formula One Club I wouldn't have got together with my husband and wouldn't have my two sons!

In June of this year another event occurs that changes the music scene in England forever, it goes down in history as "Battle of the Beanfield", we let Alan Lodge describe the events of that day. People don't like travellers we lower their house prices but we hadn't shown any violence. The police had previous, but the Stonehenge ambush was caught on camera and Dixon of Dock Green don't do this kind of thing, so there were articles as far away as the Tehran Times.

Battle of Beanfield

The first free festival I went to was in the Queens back garden at Windsor in 1972. Basically, you're hanging out with your mates and everyone's smiling. That carried on until 1974, when 600 Thames Valley police waded in. I was sat around the fire with a cup of tea when suddenly-whoop! A truncheon round the head. We got the message, we were scared stiff, so the Peoples free festival moved to Stonehenge.

I could see the way the wind was changing so I became an ambulance man and got involved with an organisation set up to help youngsters who had got into trouble with the law. First in tents then in tepee's, and then on buses and trucks, people were now permanently meandering around the country. I had a cottage in Wales with my wife and two kids and we were out and about for roughly nine months of the year.

By 1984 there were 30,000 to 40,000 people at Stonehenge living in tents. Everything you look for in human exchange was there: lack of greed, co-operation, looking out for each other, breaking down mental barriers. Bartering was important. People were grateful for me being an ambulance man: "can I do your shopping? Can I look after your kids? Everything you think about being a better society was there in the Anarchists Free State at Stonehenge".

On our way there next year we were given papers by the police outside of Salisbury stating that we'd be arrested if we went to Stonehenge because of an injunction they had taken out. We were used to this-the existence of the travelling life is an offence but we didn't know they'd assembled 1,600 policemen on our route. The convoy stopped adjacent to the famous Bean-field, well outside the five-mile radius of the court order, so I hopped out of the cab to take some pictures. Suddenly I saw this black cloud coming down the lane, a load of coppers with riot shields. They went up to the motors, many with kids in, and were whacking them with their sticks. Two pregnant ladies were dragged out through the broken windscreens by their hair. The screams are with me now.

Rather than let them come our way we turned and drove through the hedge into the field by the road. For the next five hours there was a stand-off, skirmishes continued with people trying to get out of the field. I tried to liaise with the senior policemen, but there attitude was, "we're going to arrest you all". I'm bandaging bleeding heads, but then there's truncheon wounds where you can see the skull and I'm getting nervous of people dying. So we get them out on a Wiltshire ambulance.

At seven in the evening all the coppers boiled onto the field, smashing up the vehicles and arresting people, ITN were there and took footage of the level of violence. The operation just wasn't about arresting people, but also a decommissioning exercise", hitting people so hard and ruining their homes so they'll think twice about leading this lifestyle. Overall 520 were arrested and spread around police stations up and down the country for three days, the biggest single number since the Second World War.

The charge was obstruction of the police, which is one up from a parking ticket. The government was cheering from the sidelines. Douglas Hurd said we resembled a bunch of medieval brigands.

In 1986 Parliament passed an act which criminalised twelve vehicles gathering on common land to reside. So we'd gather, stay up all night and have a rave instead.

In 1994 Michaels Howard's act made this impossible, then this last lot pass a law that means a traveller parked on the edge of a housing estate is involved in anti social behaviour.

So now a lot of people are shoved into the city where the community splits up, they can't support each other and the kids have chips on their shoulders. The return to the cities hastened the use of serious drugs.

The outcome of these acts made it impossible to have free festivals, so now welcome to the "Family Festival", where you pay hundreds of pounds to listen to music and sleep in a tent.

Since Rock and Roll broke onto the music scene in the '50s the establishment in London and local councils across the country did everything in their power to prevent teenagers from listening and dancing to music.

They would raid clubs on the pretence that they were overcrowded, people were under age and drinking, they were taking recreational drugs instead of alcohol. They didn't have the correct dance licence and when this proved futile with the explosion of pop festivals, they changed the law.

The BBC was still paying lip service to the millions of teenagers, despite their charter which stated, "That it has a duty to cater for all the public".

In 1982 ITV launched "The Tube" a brand new pop programme for teenagers which was broadcast from Newcastle upon Tyne, live every Friday tea time. It would run from the 5th November 1982 for 121 episodes until the 26th April 1987, its two main presenters being Jools Holland and Paula Yates. This one programme launched the careers of dozens of pop groups.

By the early 80's Radio One was allowed to play more pop music during the day, but old habits die hard when in 2011 the BBC faced cuts for the first time ever. They decided to bring in an outsider from an independent radio station to give them advice. He was duly shown around the Radio One 'Silo' and on entering one of the offices it was explained to him. "The people in here prepare the three minute news bulletin that goes out every hour". "How many work in here then?" he asked, "54 came back the answer", "oh my god" he said, and this is the country's leading music radio station for young people.

He never did ask how many people work for the BBC, travelling the country to listen to new up and coming music. He did go on to explain that there are a lot of talented individuals at the BBC wanting to create more music orientated programmes for teenagers. As they move up the organisation they soon come across a mushroom cloud of managers all vying to sit on top of the mushroom.

Live Aid

On July 13th 1985, Live Aid was broadcast from Wembley Stadium live around the world; it is the brain child of Bob Geldof of Boom Town Rats fame. It would go on to raise over $100 million for the starving people of Ethiopia and also put back on the political agenda the starving people of Africa.

On August bank holiday Sunday, 30 local bands appeared at Herringthorpe Stadium as the musicians of Rotherham, lead by 'Suburban Dream's' Mark Lynam staged their own version of Live Aid, it would go on to raise over £2000, with tickets at £1. The sound system was provided by local entrepreneur "John Pye" the owner of Rotherham's music store Keyboards Plus; it had just arrived back in town after being used for several months by the Eurythmics and the rock band The Alarm! On the 9th March 2011 the BBC World Service claimed that over 95% of the money raised by Live Aid was diverted by the rebels in Ethiopia to buy weapons. Bob Geldof threatened legal action if they refused to retract their story. Old Habits die hard in the BBC.

On the 5th December Steve Wright of Radio One was the DJ for the night at Peppermint Park.

Early in 1986 after a doorman was severely beaten up outside the club, the clubs licence was withdrawn.

As Keith Wilson describes "Our licence was withdrawn due to pressure from the locals, so naturally I appealed and got a barrister on the case. At appeal we were expecting our licence to be moved back to midnight from 1 am but due to the local pressure and the police we lost, no licence no night club". He now recalls," Looking back after 25 years, I think that when we had the licence extended to 1 am it sounded the death knell of the club, I had to go to

the club that same night and tell all the staff that they had lost their jobs".

His wife remembers Keith arriving home that day, "he walked in and told me the bad news, he then went straight to bed for 24 hours, still fully dressed, we were all devastated, and our livelihood had gone". When he did eventually get out of bed, Keith remembers he still had to find an income for his young family. "I looked in the small ads in the Sheffield Star and noticed someone was looking for a partner to manufacture safety containers for solvents that are used in garages. So I met them and went into a new venture". His company now employs over 20 people and has a turnover of £10 million.

As Keith Wilson sets off to become a millionaire, the Stag Roundabout had lost a club that had been home to tens of thousands of teenagers over 18 years; the equivalent of six full time jobs had been lost, the local community had lost a venue that had been used for countless private parties from people across

South Yorkshire. It had also funded numerous students through college and university, helped couples save the mortgage for a house and helped people to save and set up their own businesses. But for all the teenagers who went, their memories will always live on. So we will leave the last words to the person who in his own words changed the way we all dance, Chubby Checker. "Come along with me, to a place just down the street, where the kids are moving dancing grooving to the uptown beat of the Discotheque"

The Verdict.

How a club managed to stay open for 18 years in a residential area can only be put down to Dave Allen and later Keith Wilson, when you consider it was only licensed for 174 people but would on most weekends attract 300 plus is testament to how popular it always was. The club is now a Dance School for young children.

Dave Allen today

About the author:

Keith Brisland was born in Sheffield in 1953. He left school at 15 and become a miner and then a steelworker. His interest in the Charade stems from frequenting the club from 1970 until 1976. These days he still lives just a few hundred yards away from the building that once housed the venue

Acknowledgements

Rotherham Archives and Local Studies Services.
Rotherham Advertiser.
Sheffield Star.

Thomas McQuillin, Margaret Jackson, Matthew Ridsdale, Clifton History Group (Peter Hawkridge), Keith Hunter, Des Pejko, Judith and Anna McQuillin, Bob Holyman, Kev Brisco, Pete Horsley, Aiden and Harry Brisland, John Rose, Dave Growns, Eric Dewsnapp, Matchy, Martin Scott, Ivor Hillman, Paul Douglas, John Benson, Kathryn Brisland and Blues and Soul Magazine.

All interviews and research material will be kept in the Library at Rotherham Archives

Sue from Selby

John Rose, Charade manager (Centre) with doormen circa 1974

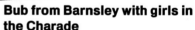

Bar staff in the Charade

Bub from Barnsley with girls in the Charade

Mods and skinheads from the Charade at Skegness in 1971 - note former Chief Constable of West Yorkshire Police Sir Norman Bettison (second row from top - second from right)